Aimé Césaire

Twayne's World Authors Series
Caribbean Literature

David O'Connell, Editor
Georgia State University

TWAS 821

Aimé Césaire in 1945. Photograph courtesy of the Service de Presse et d'Information, the French Embassy, Paris.

Aimé Césaire

Janis L. Pallister

Bowling Green State University

Twayne Publishers • New York

Maxwell Macmillan Canada • Toronto

Maxwell Macmillan International • New York Oxford Singapore Sydney

Aimé Césaire
Janis L. Pallister

Twayne Publishers   Maxwell Macmillan Canada, Inc.
Macmillan Publishing Company   1200 Eglinton Avenue East
866 Third Avenue   Suite 200
New York, New York 10022   Don Mills, Ontario M3C 3N1

Macmillan Publishing Company is part of the Maxwell Communication
Group of Companies.

Library of Congress Cataloging-in-Publication Data

Pallister, Janis L.
      Aimé Césaire / Janis L. Pallister.
           p.   cm. – (Twayne's world authors series; TWAS 821)
      Includes bibliographical references and index.
      ISBN 0-8057-8266-4 (alk. paper)
      1. Césaire, Aimé – Criticism and interpretation. I. Title. II. Series.
PQ3949.C44Z84 1991
841 – dc20   91-37155
                                                               CIP

The paper used in this publication meets the minimum requirements of
American National Standard for Information Sciences – Permanence of
Paper for Printed Library Materials, ANSI Z39.48-1984. ∞™

10 9 8 7 6 5 4 3 2 1

Printed in the United States of America

For Kathryn

If we are blessed in this world
it is in feeling this –
i.e., there are circumstances
and you are asked to be
their member

– Christopher Gilbert

Contents

Preface

This book is primarily intended for the student of world literature and as an introduction to Aimé Césaire's work. For this reason it describes Césaire's poetry collections, plays, and notable essays and places him in the groundbreaking movements of negritude and surrealism to which he has adhered in most of his writings. It also seeks to assess the critical trends that have arisen in connection with this major black Martinique writer. I hope to have identified new areas of investigation and to have offered new conclusions about Césaire's career in regard to the breadth of his work, his putative misogyny, and the relevance of negritude today.

In view of Césaire's concerns with slavery, racism, and colonialism, it is no surprise that the two dominant themes of his work should come to be identified as the need for revolution and the cry for decolonization. While examining these themes in all Césaire's works, I also discuss the works as products of a particular human condition, both in a historical context and in that of the twentieth-century social, cultural, and political milieu to which they pertain. My approach to Césaire's work is chronological and developmental, and I have assumed little or no knowledge of French on the part of the reader. I give a synopsis of or describe each work and then discuss its significance and the major criticism, but I also assess the work myself.

In this book I have dealt with the critical literature pertaining to Césaire selectively. Because so much text has been devoted to negritude in general and Césaire in particular, I have opted to concentrate on the texts themselves and to inform the reader of the principal critical trends pertinent to these texts. In the Selected Bibliography readers will find both French- and English-language editions of Césaire's work and abundant secondary material in both languages.

This book, then, claims in no way to be definitive or exhaustive; rather, it seeks to provide an introduction for the uninitiated inquirer and a quick reference work for the seasoned scholar. I also

hope to provide new insights or articulations that may yet be further
developed and explored, either by me or by some other reader of
Aimé Césaire.

* * *

I wish to thank Dr. Ramona Cormier and Dr. Ellen Berry for their
kind assistance in reviewing the text, and Naaman Editions for permission to reprint excerpts from *Cahier d'un retour au pays natal*
that I translated in *The Bruised Reed*. Quotations from the Seuil
French-language version of *Cahier d'un retour au pays natal* and
from Marie Collins's translation of this work are used with the kind
permission of these parties. Permission to include additional quotations from *Cahier d'un retour au pays natal, Discours sur le colonialisme,* and *Toussaint Louverture* has been granted by Présence
Africaine. The frontispiece photograph is used by permission of the
Service de Presse et d'Information, the French Embassy. For his gen-
erous interventions and assistance, I am also grateful to Professor
David O'Connell.

Chronology

1834	Césaire's ancestor, perhaps a freed slave, is arrested for having been involved in the insurrection in Grand-Anse, Martinique, in 1833.
1843-1848	The slaves of Martinique are freed by Victor Schoelcher.
1868	Fernand Césaire, Aimé's paternal grandfather, is born.
1913	Aimé Césaire is born 25 June in Basse-Pointe, Martinique.
1919	Enters primary school in Basse-Pointe.
1924	Enters the Lycée Victor Schoelcher in Fort-de-France. Gilbert Gratiant, Octave Mannoni, E. Revert, and Louis Achille are his professors; Léon-Gontran Damas is a classmate.
1932	Arrives in Paris in September.
1932-1933	Enters the Lycée Louis-le-Grand as a student; meets Ousmane Soucé and Léopold Sédar Senghor.
1933-1934	Attains full entrance to Lycée Louis-le-Grand; studies philosophy (Husserl, Heidegger, Jaspers, Kierkegaard) under René Le Senne.
1934	With Damas and Senghor founds the review *L'Etudiant noir;* in it publishes an article in which the word *negritude* appears, evidently for the first time.
1935	Is accepted into the Ecole Normale Supérieure. Travels to Dalmatia with his friend Petar Guberina. Returning to Paris, begins writing *Cahier d'un retour au pays natal,* ostensibly preceded by a novel set in the Antilles, portraying a rather misogynist hero.

1936   With Senghor reads and discusses the writings of the
            ethnologist Leo Frobenius, whose *History of African
            Civilization* has just been translated into French and
            published by Gallimard.

1937   Marries Suzanne Roussy.

1939   *Cahier d'un retour au pays natal* published in the
            review *Volontés*. Césaire returns to Martinique three
            days after the beginning of World War II on 1
            September. He, along with his wife, begins teaching
            at the Lycée Victor Schoelcher. Two of his most dis-
            tinguished pupils are Edouard Glissant and Frantz
            Fanon.

1941   The review *Tropiques* is founded. André Breton visits
            Martinique and becomes aware of the literary scene
            there. Following his visit, the review begins to cham-
            pion the surrealist movement.

1944   *Cahier d'un retour au pays natal*, with a preface by
            Breton, is published in a bilingual format by Editions
            Hémisphères and reprinted in the review *Fontaine*.
            Césaire travels and lectures in Haiti. Publication by
            Gallimard of *Les Armes miraculeuses*, containing
            some poems that had already appeared in *Tropiques*,
            as well as the poetry version of *Et les chiens se tai-
            saient*, inspired by recent reading of Nietzsche's es-
            say on Greek tragedy.

1945   Becomes mayor of Fort-de-France and is elected
            deputy of the Communist party to the National As-
            sembly.

1946   As deputy of Martinique, presents papers containing
            a request that Martinique and Guadeloupe become
            overseas departments of France; request is granted
            and becomes legal on 19 March. He stipulates that
            certain concessions be made to the special cultures
            of these departments (as well as of Réunion and
            Guyana).

1948 Participates in the founding of the journal *Présence africaine*, which has Alioune Diop as its editor. Publication by Le Quadrangle of third volume of poetry, *Soleil cou coupé* (which will reappear in 1961 as part of *Cadastre*). Senghor publishes his landmark *Anthologie de la nouvelle poésie nègre et malgache*, to which Jean-Paul Sartre will join his famous essay "Orphée noir." This anthology broadens awareness of the negritude movement to an international scope.

1949 Publication of the collection *Corps perdu*, parts of which will be revised and republished in *Cadastre*.

1950 The 64-page essay *Discours sur le colonialisme*, in part a critique of Mannoni's *Psychologie de la colonisation* and having much in common with some of the writings of Frantz Fanon, published by Editions Réclame (other editions appear in 1953, 1955, and 1970). First edition of *Corps perdu* published by Editions Fragrance (containing 32 engravings by Picasso).

1956 *Et les chiens se taisaient* published as a theatrical arrangement by Présence Africaine. Césaire publishes *Art poétique* with Seghers and participates in the First International Congress of Black Writers, in Paris, presenting the paper "Culture et colonisation." Formally splits with the Communist party and explains this step in *Lettre à Maurice Thorez*. In his preface to Daniel Guérin's *Antilles décolonisées* he expresses his growing concern with the negative results of departmentalization, which threatens Caribbean culture.

1959 At the Second International Congress of Black Writers, in Rome, gives the paper "L'Homme de culture et ses responsabilités." Also publishes the essay "La Pensée politique de Sékou Touré" in *Présence africaine.*

1960   *Ferrements* is published by Seuil and wins the Prix René Laporte (eight of its poems have previously been published in *Présence africaine*, between 1955 and 1959).

1961   *Cadastre* published; it contains *Soleil cou coupé* and *Corps perdu*. The historical study *Toussaint Louverture* published by Présence Africaine.

1962   *Et les chiens se taisaient* translated into Italian as a "lyrical oratorio."

1963   Publication by Présence Africaine of the play *La Tragédie du roi Christophe*.

1964   The Jean-Marie Serreau company presents *Christophe* in several cities around the world: Paris, Brussels, Salzburg, Berlin.

1965   The play *Une saison au Congo* published; it, too, will be presented by the Jean-Marie Serreau company in Paris (1967) and will also be performed in a suburb of Brussels.

1969   The play *Une tempête* is published by Seuil. It is presented in Tunisia by Serreau and in Martinique by Yvan Labejof.

1976   *Oeuvres complètes* published by Désormeaux in Fort-de-France. This three-volume collection includes the first publication of 17 poems under the title *Noria*.

1982   *Moi, laminaire* published by Seuil.

1985   Attends first international colloquy on his work, 21-23 November.

1987   The poem "Configurations" is published in *Aimé Césaire, ou l'athanor d'un alchimiste*, a collection of essays originally read at a 1985 international colloquy on his work. Césaire's collected works appear in German translation by Brigitte Weidmann.

1990   Is part of an official municipal reception of the Conseil International des Etudes Francophones, Fort-de-France.

Introduction

One of the three pioneers of the negritude movement, Aimé Césaire was born 25 June 1913 in Basse-Pointe, Martinique. In his book-length autobiographical poem, *Cahier d'un retour au pays natal* (1939; *Notebook of a Return to My Native Land*), he describes his childhood, spent in a small, rat-infested house that sheltered his six brothers and sisters, a father who seemed to be constantly consumed by sorrow, and his mother, forever laboring at her Singer sewing machine to earn enough money so that her family would not go hungry.

Despite such poverty, however, Césaire, with the poet Léon-Gontran Damas, was able to enter Fort-de-France's Lycée Victor Schoelcher in 1924 and graduate from this rather distinguished secondary school in 1931. Like the most talented of Martinique's youth, he soon found himself embarked for the *Métropole*, already crammed with a great deal of knowledge about France and its culture, as was so characteristic of the colonial education received by French subjects of the period.

The celebrated Martiniquais philosopher Frantz Fanon well depicts this scenario in his *Black Skin, White Masks* (1952). The young person about to depart for France is able to read his "power" and "transformation" in the eyes of those who have accompanied him to the dock, where he will board the ship for the magic land of Paris, the Sorbonne, the rue Pigalle.[1] One imagines the young Césaire's departure as something like Fanon's description. Yet once installed in Paris and attending first the Lycée Louis-le-Grand (1932-33) and then the Ecole Normale Supérieure (which he entered in 1935), Césaire must surely have led a life different from that of the average West Indian student, for in Paris he was to meet the Senegalese Léopold Sédar Senghor and again the French Guyanan Damas, who with Césaire launched the negritude movement for which the three became world famous.

Through Senghor Césaire learned of African traditions and

values that had not only been lost to New World blacks but also often intentionally obliterated by slave owners and colonizers. These new ideas fed Césaire's dislike for and alienation from colonial Martinique. The small review *L'Etudiant noir*, which launched the concept of negritude, was founded by Césaire, Senghor, and Damas. Though short-lived (September 1934 to 1936), it was instrumental in providing a forum for interaction between blacks of the Antilles and those of Africa.

Stemming from his relationship with Senghor and his experience with *L'Etudiant noir* – whose antecedents lay in the works of such writers of the American Harlem Renaissance as Langston Hughes and Claude McKay and in periodicals like the *Légitime Défense* (founded in 1932 and having only six issues) – Césaire's anticolonialist beliefs were soon recorded in the first drafts of his *Cahier d'un retour au pays natal*. In this blistering outcry Césaire expressed his anger at the conditions of his race in Martinique – and throughout the world for that matter. The poem also articulated the tenets of negritude and incidentally evoked the flora and fauna of Martinique. (Such evocations of Africa had been one of the hallmarks of René Maran's *Batouala*, a forerunner of negritude, which won the Prix Goncourt in 1922. Maran had also evoked African language through his insertion of certain expressions, interspersed throughout the dialogue; Césaire and Senghor were to do likewise.) Césaire's poem was republished in 1944 by Editions Hémisphères with a preface by André Breton and has been revised by Césaire several times. It went largely unnoticed in the Europe of the 1940s, although it does seem to have been read in Africa and the West Indies, for by 1947 the negritude poets were already "there." At any rate, *Cahier d'un retour* is of prime importance both in the story of the poet's life and in the history of literature, for, as Jack Corzani states, this work, like all Césaire's poetry, is a cathartic – it has a therapeutic value not only for Césaire but for all his black readers.[2]

Returning to Martinique in 1939, Césaire pursued literary interests while teaching at the Lycée Victor Schoelcher in Fort-de-France, as did his wife, the writer Suzanne Roussy, a Martiniquaise whom he married in 1937 and who collaborated with him and Senghor on *L'Etudiant noir*. In 1940-41 he, with his wife; his friends René Ménil, Aristide Maugée, Georges Gratiant; and other young writers, founded the review *Tropiques*, which by its call for change in the social order and its critique of the Nazi's Vichy government in Paris caused some trouble for Césaire but also established him as a political leader. (It was through this review that Breton became aware of Césaire.) Accordingly, by 1945 he was elected a delegate to the National Assembly in Paris, as well as mayor of Fort-de-France, a post he has occupied for more than four decades. His affiliation with Martinique's Communist party (an arm of the one in France) no doubt explains his political success: once elected, he fought for Martinique to become an overseas *département* of France, a goal realized in 1946. (The Communists believed that this status would give the Martiniquais greater power in the political system.) Césaire founded the Parti Progressiste Martiniquais at this point and became its president. He remained a registered member of the Communist party for 14 years.

In 1944 came the next collection of poetry, *Les Armes miraculeuses* (*Miraculous weapons*), which included a poetry version of *Et les chiens se taisaient* (*And the Dogs Were Silent*), followed in 1948 by *Soleil cou coupé* (*Beheaded Sun*). From 1949 to 1960 he published two more collections of poetry, *Corps perdu* (1949; *Lost Body*) and *Ferrements* (1960; *Shackles*). During this time he revised *Soleil cou coupé* and published it in 1961 under the title *Cadastre* (with *Corps perdu*). He also published *Et les chiens se taisaient* as a play in 1956. Césaire's poetic nature has readily adapted itself to the writing of plays, which, in addition to *Et les chiens se taisaient,* include *La Tragédie du roi Christophe* (1963; *The Tragedy of King Christophe*), *Une saison au Congo* (1965; *A Season in the Congo*), and *Une tempête* (1969; *A Tempest*).

Like many twentieth-century writers, especially black writers, Césaire exemplifies the model of *le poète engagé* (the committed poet). He has devoted his life to Martinique, this leeward island discovered by Christopher Columbus in 1502, this former French colony that once and for quite some time functioned as a slave economy but now, thanks to Césaire's efforts, is an overseas department of France. "Mine is a telluric poetry," he told Gérard Georges Pigeon in a 1977 interview; "I am marked indisputably by the natural environment of Martinique."[3] He is a poet who illustrates the theories of Gaston Bachelard in that he shows the symbolic forces of water and of the island: a land adrift, separated from the mainland physically and culturally, surrounded by mountains and ocean, beaten by the sea's violent forces but also sustained by the sea – a kind of prison, a closed system.

Césaire has consistently embraced the notion of change, of revolution, in both his literary works and his professional life as a politician. From an insular childhood that taught him the meaning of solitude, Césaire moved gradually to the adult mission of championing his island and his race on the world front. In fact, his is as much a quest for country as it is an assertion of the philosophical concept of negritude or of his aesthetics. If Césaire's art rests on hate, that hate is not so much targeted at persons as at the evil of racism and discrimination. His poetry carries with it the reproach of such evil, for as Jean Wagner shows us in quite another context, personal purification and moral elevation can be derived from hate, at least from the kind of hate we are speaking of here.[4]

It is, however, ironic that by 1956 Césaire had lost his earlier enthusiasm about departmentalization. Yet there was good reason for him to doubt the efficacy of the change, for the manner in which French laws came to be applied to the former colony left it basically little changed: France's assimilationist regard for the Martiniquais made the island still fundamentally colonial. Where some ills of this colonial dinosaur were corrected by departmentalization, others sprang up in their place, for as Susan Frutkin writes, "French policies retained the stigma and the essence of abhorrent colonialism."[5] As a result, Césaire moved from a position that strongly advocated departmentalization to one that embraced the right of self-determination. This time at the end of the war when hope and equality engendered such ideas as departmentalization Beverley Ormerod calls a period of myth.[6] Needless to say, disenchantment with departmentalization is prevalent.

This position is in fact deeply woven into Césaire's antirationalist, anti-European, antiassimilationist philosophy, which has been richly fed by his association with Senghor and by his reading of the Harlem Renaissance poets and the French poets Arthur Rimbaud and Lautréamont, not to mention the surrealists. Moreover, that same position underscores the fact that Césaire's brush with communism was much briefer and certainly much more ambiguous than is often contended. Early on, he became aware of the connection between the Communist party and the mentality of the assimilationists. His creative writings are far more oriented toward all forms of anticolonialism than toward any doctrinaire political stance or party. Frutkin views Césaire's negritude as incompatible with communism; she also rightly asserts that he is a poet first and a politician second. Ormerod discusses Césaire's connections with communism, saying that the Césaire of 1956 inevitably broke with communism when the Soviet Union invaded Hungary. But there were other reasons as well, having to do in great part with Césaire's realization that the Communists were hardly more removed from imperialist, dictatorial, repressive, and assimilationist goals than were the non-Communists.

Even though certain passages in his texts often seem to echo Karl Marx's *Yearbook,* Césaire repudiated communism rather sooner than later – as did many an intellectual, Jean-Paul Sartre included. One must suppose that such repudiation does not necessarily mean the scrapping of Marxist philosophy part and parcel, or of the social and economic philosophy Marx reveled in. For him philosophy was Promethean and atheistic. And Césaire, after all an independent thinker, does not concur with all Marxist doctrine. Nevertheless, neither the insistence on the need for economic and social change nor the notion that the victims of history ultimately seize control of it is alien to Césaire. We should note, however, that according to Keith O. Tribble, Césaire's reception by Soviet critics has been determined by his defection (1957-60) from the French Communist party, although the publication of *Une saison au Congo* did contribute to a superficial reconciliation of the poet with the Soviets.[7] (The Congolese Patrice Lumumba is a hero in the Soviet Union, where a university is named in his honor.)

It is essentially within this framework that we should observe the man of action Césaire has been, both as National Assembly delegate and mayor of Fort-de-France. It is also within this framework that we see him producing a long list of philosophical and theoretical writings that begin with the all-important 1950 essay *Discours sur le colonialisme* (*Discourse on Colonialism*). In 1956 came *Lettre à Maurice Thorez* (*Letter to Maurice Thorez*), in which he rejected Communist ideology, followed by the essays "Culture et colonisation" (1956; "Culture and Colonization"), "L'Homme de culture et ses responsabilités" (1959; "The Man of Culture and His Responsibilites"), and "Crise dans les départments d'outremer" (1961; "Crisis in the Overseas Departments"); the historical study

Toussaint Louverture (1961); the essay "La Grandeur de Lumumba était de nier la réalité" (1966; "The Greatness of Lumumba Was to Deny Reality"); and many other essays, published in *Le Monde*, *Présence africaine*, and elsewhere. (The most important of these essays are analyzed in chapter 7.)

We are confronted with many problems in regard to Césaire's biography. On the most fundamental facts of his life, dates vary from one author to another: his birth date is variously given as 1912 and 1913, for instance. Perhaps the most useful book with respect to Césaire's life is Mbawil a Mpaang Ngal's *Aimé Césaire: Un Homme à la recherche d'une patrie*,[8] for here the facts are interwoven with the evolution of the poet's way of thinking. We can also more readily trace this evolution by examining what he has read. Those writers who contributed to the poet's transformation include the novelist and politician Maurice Barrès *(Les Déracinés);* the poets Rimbaud, Lautréamont, and Guillaume Apollinaire; ethnologists like Leo Frobenius,[9] Lucien Lévy-Bruhl, and Godfrey H. Hardy (not to mention those he might refute, particularly the French theoretician of racism[10] Arthur de Gobineau); and social philosophers, especially Marx. Obviously, the influence of Senghor is both literary and personal, as may also be said of Damas and Breton. Césaire's relations with artists like André Masson and Wilfredo Lam must be of some account here too. Césaire's absorption of all his readings – be they surrealist, Communist, revolutionary, Marxist, anticolonialist; be they theoretical or creative, philosophical or poetic – when coupled with his life experiences is what informs his works. And these influences would also include his early exposures to *écriture* and *lecture* (reading) at the knee of his strict tax-collector father, who read to his children from the French classics.

These diverse currents help explain the aesthetics of liberation and the use of hatred as a revolutionary tool: these are the hallmarks of Césaire's poetic and political style. Césaire – not unlike Rimbaud, with his *poète-visionnaire,* or even Paul Claudel, with his *poète-prêtre* – sees the poet as *poète-sentinelle,* one who shares the condition of his people but is also an instrument of protection and forewarning. In Césaire's poetry, dedicated to this cause, one may observe a tension revolving around certain axes. There is a striking pull between concepts of time – past, present, and future, or night and day – as well as between the poles of death and life. There is a constant return to the conflicting agendas of master and slave, of colonizer and colonized. Similarly, movement in space is sometimes horizontal, sometimes vertical; the geography floats and shifts, in the poetry as well as the plays.

In the following pages I explain what Césaire can mean by the word *negritude,* a word he coined and Senghor adopted and helped to define, a word now in *Webster's* dictionary. Césaire's contribution to black and world literature is far-reaching. We may regard him as a Francophone poet, a black poet from the Antilles, or a chief contributor to the surrealist movement on the Continent, although his surrealism (or surrealist modernism) is tied to his negritude. In either or in both cases, our understanding of his impact is vital, for his works are read and studied the world over. His influence in Italy, the Soviet Union, and French Canada has been demonstrated by several contemporary scholars, including Jack Corzani, Graziano Benelli, Keith Tribble, and Roger and Max Dorsinville,[11] and his plays have been performed worldwide, *La Tragédie du roi Christophe* having been staged in Venice as early as September 1964.

In choosing the angle from which to approach Césaire's writing we are also confronted with the problem of which critical approach will best suit his and other African-American and African poetry or, for that matter, any literature of the African continuum. Many contend that no European approach, not even the Marxist-Goldmanian-Lukacsian approach,[12] is appropriate to an analysis of this literature. In this book, therefore, I have followed a textual and epitextual treatment insofar as possible, acknowledging the hazards of viewing this work with Western eyes but realizing that Westerners have no other eyes with which to do so.

Chapter One

Return

Cahier d'un retour au pays natal – the title alone tells us much. It informs us of the poem's modernity: it says the poem is a "notebook" – certainly not a formal or traditional genre. It speaks of return, after many physical voyages the world over, after many spiritual voyages in which the native land has been spurned as a source of embarrassment. Not only return but *a* return, and a significant one. An archetypal return or *nostos,* one not unlike that of the prodigal son. A return to the land of one's birth; a return that marks the end of alienation and the beginning of an identity with one's compatriots, with those of one's own race and culture.

The title suggests resolution rather than the "heart of a conflict," as André Breton has said. It is interesting to note in this respect that the poem, which ultimately came to have some 1,055 lines, was no doubt begun as early as 1936, just as Césaire was completing his studies at the Ecole Normale Supérieure and preparing to go back to Martinique. It can be looked at as the product of his long meditation on being black and on the condition of the black race, sustained during his years in Paris when he exchanged ideas with Senghor, Damas, and others and read voraciously. It is, among other things, a journal of how Césaire's shame evolved into pride.

In the *Cahier* Césaire traces this dolorous journey – both his and that of his race – in all its anguish, tensions, positionings, passion (or suffering), and ecstasy. Mbawil a Mpaang Ngal maintains that, in the *Cahier,* the poet aims to re-create the drama and the condition of the black in time (historical and present time) and space, imagining where the black may be after the diaspora – that is, the scattering of the black race over the world – for, as he says, no race has traveled as much as the black. The work, says Ngal, is "like a social ceremony, a reactualization of the history of his race" (Ngal, 67). But it is also a history of his own person, of his own maturation, which is, in many

1

respects, the same history as that of all Caribbean blacks. As Jacques Chevrier says, Césaire recognizes himself here as the bastard of the Antilles.[1] Europe, his father, denies him. Africa, his mother, denies him. Indeed, the personal history is fused to the history of the race, so that we encounter the waif, the child, chewing on his sugarcane root, who, having become a man, is pictured with a rope around his neck, being dragged down a bloody road or standing in the "ring"–the ring of the entertainer, the gladiator, with the "revolutionary" (black martyrs and leaders) tossed to the lions. Thus, while speaking of his own experience, Césaire also gives a new identity to, a new definition of the black.

At the very onset of this poem, with its floating geography, which fixes the Antilles and Africa as the sites of world hunger, starvation, and misery and yet as the loci of an unequalled humanism, we learn how negritude had its beginnings. It was in Haiti where negritude rose up in rebellion for the first time and declared its belief in its own humanity. Without looking outside the poem we see that one of the attributes of negritude is to revolt against that which dehumanizes. The allusion is, of course, to the revolution Toussaint Louverture mounted in Haiti (then Saint-Domingue) in Napoleonic times, and the specter of Toussaint, the story of his achievements and his ultimate passion at the hands of his French jailers, will haunt these pages.[2] It is written in what Césaire would claim to be the blood and sweat of the entire race. It takes issue with the ways of the West, which he views as rationalist, exploitative, and hypocritical.

On the surface the poem appears to be an autobiography as well. Told in the first person, the work seems from the outset to be a narrative poem, a story told by a poet to a hypothetical listener. The persona speaks of his early experiences in which he had turned away from his island and his race, but he also tells us how in the final stages of his spiritual journey he turned toward "lost paradises." These can be the lost paradises of Africa and its culture, paradises lost to him and to his people. It was by that experience, he tells us, that he liberated the lyricism deep within himself.

We can set 1939 as the date of the first printed version of this poem, appearing in what Breton calls "a Paris journal" but one that Maryse Condé identifies as *Volontés*.[3] Since then the work has gone through many revisions. It has in fact been the concerted effort of Thomas Hale to show all the many dates of its evolution and subsequent publications.[4] Ronnie Scharfman seems to belittle this approach, but in reality she overlooks the fact that serious problems are implicit in this constant refashioning of the text.[5] Hale has shown that in the 1939 version only 75 percent of the poem was present. We may speak of the 1956 Présence Africaine edition as the "definitive edition," but the poem in *Volontés* is not the poem of the Présence Africaine edition. That which Césaire has added to the 1939 text does not make up a "definitive" text but a different one. As long as Césaire lives, he can still add more (and this too constitutes a kind of constant "return" and refashioning). And so we must inevitably ask ourselves, Which is the text? Which text shall we use?

Leaving this textual difficulty aside, we ask ourselves, Who is the *je* of this poem, this story told to the reader(s) in the first person? We no doubt ought to understand that the use of the first-person singular in the *Cahier d'un retour*, as in *Les Armes miraculeuses*, forms an expression of collectivity: here *je* ("I") in reality equals *nous* ("we"), and *mon* ("my") equals *notre* ("ours"), as is the case in much neo-African literature. Thus, subjectivity or autobiographical modes are seldom if at all present in Césaire's creative writings, as – for somewhat different reasons, but with similar results – they are likewise absent from both ancient and pre-Cartesian European literature, including the essays of Montaigne. Whereas knowledge and understanding of the self per se, or of the self as the source of knowledge of the self, was absent in European literature before the evolution of the *cogito* as identified by Descartes, in the literature of the African continuum it is necessary that the artist put function before all other considerations, and so, as Janheiz Jahn says, the created poem (or mask) takes on the power of the matter that generated it in order to perform as might a seed.[6] It will express the essence of matter, which is the poet, and still more importantly the thoughts, needs, and emotions of the collectivity. Yet curiously enough it is the polis (in Montaigne, humanity) that in both cases speaks through the artist's breath and voice, through his or her creation. Can it be for this proprietary reason that Ali Mazrui, in speaking of negritude in his controversial television series "The Africans," feels free to quote several lines from the Caribbean poet's *Cahier d'un retour* without feeling any compulsion to identify his source?

It is this generalized "I" that allows Breton to state that the poem transcends the anguish of the black man and embraces the most unbearable yet also the most repairable aspects of the human condition as created by society.[7] That this society can be changed is an arm of Césaire's humanism but one less often studied than might be wished. One might add that although the *je* is present from the first sentence of the poem, at times it is suppressed, as if by such suppression the *je* might be generalized, as is the *tu* of the poem. *Tu* ("you," singular, familiar) is *autrui*, the other person, the reader, the listener, the recipient, the one who sees the mask. Later in the poem, however, when the poet returns to his island – where he had found death, pettiness, greed, absurdity, futility, disease – the words "moi seul" ("I alone"; *Cahier*, 63-65) take on a somewhat different aura. Solitude is implied by the expression, but also implied is the recognition of a prophetic mission: "I the outcast have returned; I only am escaped alone to tell thee" (Job 1:15-19); I have escaped the wreck so that I might give an account of disaster. I am – like Ishmael the father-seeker, the son of Rachel – the sole survivor of the wreck. (Something of *The Tempest* seems also involved here.) And the poet goes on to tell his difficulty in counting himself as part of the world. He has the sense of being cut off from the cool oases of brotherhood. It is this self-conceptualization, at once personal and mythic – of the proportions of the hero and a story coming from the mythos or mouth – that introduces that great reclamation. Now he is prepared to take back the Caribbean, the archipelago, the Antilles as African continuum, and to declare his confraternity with the world Negro, who has built the modern city, mined the mines, amused the Americans with his tap dancing and his jazz, and undergone lynchings in the American South. My translated excerpts in *The Bruised Reed* make clear this geographical sweep:

> Unquestionably mine are these few thousand souls necrosed by mortification who dance about in the calabash of an island, and mine too the archipelago arched like the troubled desire to deny itself, like a mother's anxiety to protect the more delicate tenuousness which separates one of the Americas from the other; and its flanks which secrete for Europe the sweet liquors of a Gulf Stream, and one of the two incandescent passages between which the Equator walks the tightrope to Africa. And mine this unenclosed island, its bright audacity reared up at the back of this polynesia; in front of it Guadeloupe, split in two by its dorsal ridge and having the same wretchedness as us, Haiti

where negritude stood up on its two feet for the first time and said it believed in its humanity, and the comical little tail of Florida where the strangling of a negro is just being finished and Africa gigantically caterpillaring up to the Spanish boot of Europe, Africa's nakedness where Death mows humans down with a wide sweep of the scythe.[8]

As the poet continues, he shows that the black and his contribution are everywhere:

> And I call myself Bordeaux and Nantes and Liverpool and New
> York and San Francisco
> not an inch of the world which does not bear my
> fingerprint . . .
>
> Virginia. Tennessee. Georgia. Alabama . . .
> absurdly muted trumpets
> Red lands, bloody lands, bloodkinship lands . . .
> (Pallister 1978, 66-67)

The poet is now prepared to sing the culture hero, in this case Toussaint. My translation in *The Bruised Reed* differs from this of Collins:

> Mine too is a small
> cell in the Jura
> a small cell, the snow doubling the cell with white bars
> the snow is a white jailer who stands
> guard before a prison.
>
> Mine too
> is a lone man imprisoned by
> white
> is a lone man who defies the
> white cries of white death
> (TOUSSAINT, TOUSSAINT
> LOUVERTURE)
> is a man who engrosses the white hawk of death
> is a lone man in the sterile sea of white sand
> is an old nigger erect against the waters of the sky
> Death describes a shining circle above this man
> death the star grazes softly over his head
> death the madwoman breathes into the ripe sugar-
> cane of his arms
> death a white horse gallops into the prison

death with its cat-eyes gleams in the shadow
death water under the Reefs' hiccoughs
death is a wounded bird
death wanes
death hesitates
death is a shadowy patyura[9]
death expires into a white pond
of silence.[10]

The speaker is by now ready to reconstruct the history of his race. And here we should digress to point out that this *prise de conscience* includes totemic identification with the tree and with the river (tropes we will find in *Christophe* and *Une saison au Congo*). It also includes the recollection of the whip of slavery. This terrible sound is commingled with the sweet sounds of the river. It includes all the recollections of childhood, good and bad. It includes the poet's (that is, the race's) confession of his (its) rejection of Western religion, particularly as urged by missionaries, and of Western-style "charity." The poet establishes in place of that religion and its charity a capitulation to an African past (dances, bedecked in feather and skins; idols). Indeed, in the presence of such, he (the race) inserts a voodoolike incantation mixed with recollections of childhood.

Here in the poem comes the celebrated condemnation of reason as a tool for knowing life (*Cahier*, 71). For the colonized, reason has been above all the instrument of rationalization, a means of justifying disorder and torture. We (I) prefer, he says, the madness of a tenacious cannibalism. What can he mean? Perhaps the cannibalism represents an attack on the conscience of the white man. We (I) prefer to gnaw at the white man's conscience, his flesh. We (I) prefer to remind him of his deeds. (For the white man has been, as Frantz Fanon says, a voracious eater of men!)[11] If reason is repudiated here it is so for a different reason than is the case with the surrealists (although Breton [*Cahier*, 25-26] would like to contend that the surrealist intention of cutting down "bon sens" is inscribed in the poem). It seems more probable that Césaire's "hatred of reason" is, as just stated, based on the racist policies "reason" has managed to generate and substantiate.

If we are not allied with Western rationalism, the poet asks, what then do "we" endorse? As suggested, we endorse the role of conscience. We endorse the positive values of negritude. We endorse poetry: the voice would be our weapon to tell all, to shout out the truth. And if poetry is our weapon, then poetry is our defense. By a somewhat circuitous path, the reader is led to the conclusion that, among other things, the passage is a defense of poetry, to which the poet has claimed his dedication, just ahead of this antirational declaration.

Once this reason is repudiated, how shall "we" find out who and what "we" are? The answer we find is perhaps the very definition of negritude. Césaire asserts that he, his negritude, is a "tree" (*Cahier*, 75), a symbol at once naturally correct (the human has all the same components of a tree) and African in its rooted-in-soil concept. Although somewhat later the poet declares "homo sum" – no matter how one measures, still later he states that his negritude is not a construct even if Western rationalism can only understand him or his essence through a construct. Rather, he says, his negritude "plonge dans la chair rouge du sol; dans la chair ardente du ciel" ("plunges into the red flesh of the soil, into the burning flesh of the sky"; *Cahier*, 117). In these lines he reprises the tree symbol, prevalent in his poetry, and especially important at the end of *Une saison au Congo*. The tree represents rectitude, erectness, nature-directedness; it represents also virility and fertility, all that is non-Western, all that is African. The primacy of the vegetal is declared; the tearing of flesh by the wicked teeth of the carnivore is somehow not in play here.

Within the context of this poem, too, and without any particular search among critics, one readily grasps the shifting of values that negritude must involve. The color white, so often associated with the good, the pure, the innocent, becomes a negative thing, while black, usually associated with the ugly and the morally reprehensible, becomes a positive thing. After his capture by the French, Toussaint Louverture is pictured as a solitary figure in his cell in the Jura – the solitary figure of the leader (as Le Rebelle in *Et les chiens se taisaient*). The subversions of traditional color imagery flood to both the poet's mind and pen, as can readily be seen in the previously quoted passage from Collins.

Equally within the context of the poem we learn – but in a passage that involves an indirect deconstruction or devaluing of Western industrialization and technocracy – that negritude involves courage, fortitude, and patience. We learn that it is the sweat and the hard, ill-paid labor of the black race that has built the world, that this race is innocent of having invented, of having been *homo faber,* of having bowed to the gods of reason and progress:

> Those who have not invented gunpowder or the
>   compass
> Those who have never been able to subdue steam
>   or electricity
> Those who have neither explored the seas or the
>   heavens
> but know the tiniest corners of the country of suffering
> those who have known only the uprooting elements
>   of travel
> those who have bent over in genuflection
> those who have been domesticated and
>   christianized
> those who have been inoculated with illegitimacy
> tom-toms of heavy hands
> inane tom-toms of sonorous wounds
> burlesque tom-toms of withering betrayal
>   Tepid dawn of ancestral warmths and fears
> my wanderer's riches overboard
> my authentic fakeness overboard.
>   (Pallister 1978, 68; ll. 58-71)

This people has not been involved in the manufacture of things, the poet declares with some pride. Rather, this race has remained rooted in the soil and has kept its contact with telluric and natural forces (and, according to Eric Sellin, its spiritual relationship with Africa,[12] as well as the fundamental animism of the black worldview):

> . . . my negritude is not a stone,
> nor deafness flung out against the vigour of the
>   day
> my negritude is not a white speck of dead water
> on the dead eye of the earth
> my negritude is neither tower nor cathedral
>
> it plunges into the red flesh of the soil
> it plunges into the blazing flesh of the sky
> my negritude riddles with holes
> the dense affliction of its worthy patience.
>   (Collins, 29; ll. 66-74)[13]

Among other things, passages such as the one above in which Césaire repeats, almost as a boast, that his race has "never invented anything" and passages in which he incorporates evocations of outstanding black historical figures such as Toussaint Louverture can be considered as direct responses to nineteenth-century concepts of race and of progress. Arthur de Gobineau, for example, in his essay "Racial Inequality," writes, "So the brain of the Huron Indian contains in an undeveloped form an intellect which is absolutely the same as that of the Englishman or the Frenchman! Why then, in the course of ages, has he not invented printing or steam power? I should be quite justified in asking our Huron why, if he is equal to our European peoples, his tribe has never produced a Caesar or a Charlemagne among its warriors, and why his bards and sorcerers have, in some inexplicable way, neglected to become Homers and Galens" (Biddiss, 71).

Negritude, we also learn, involves courage and the revolutionary fervor necessary to confront the oppressor with a sense of fraternity and a love of one's people. Negritude must be a springboard to action. The past is the past, and any emotional rooting in the past must be a source of strength for future social and political revolt, says the poet in the following passage. But he also delineates the qualities of the special leader in that same context:

> Give me the sorcerer's savage faith
> give my hands the power to mould
> my soul the temper of the sword
> I will stand firm. Make of my head a prow
> and of myself make neither a father
> nor a brother nor a son
> but the father, the brother, the son
> do not make me a husband, but the lover of this
>   unique people
>
> Make me rebellious against all vanity but docile to
>   its genius
> like the fist of our extended arm
> Make me the steward of its blood . . .
> make me a man of ending
> make me a man of beginning
> make me a man of harvesting
> but also make me a man of sowing . . .
>
> (Collins, 31-33; ll. 101-11, 113-16)

Negritude, the reaffirmation of black civilization and black values, embraces the notion that black is beautiful and that blacks' cultural and historical heritage is enormously significant. Therefore, the *Cahier* draws on layer after layer of culture. On the surface, the so-called contribution of the French people to those they have colonized is implicit in the use of the French language as the vehicle of expression for this poem. And yet the language itself, remolded, has been turned back upon the colonizer. The African substratum is also present in many parts of the poem.[14]

Most of all this is a poem about the island cultures of the Antilles, about the poverty and economic disenfranchisement of these islands; the house on the rue Paille, the street itself *une honte* ("a disgrace"; *Cahier*, 55), in vivid contrast to the street on which the colonists live, with their fine houses; la rue De Profundis, in the town of Gros-Morne, a street with the frankness, at least, to announce death's presence (*Cahier*, 95), what Césaire calls "la misère des taudis" ("the wretched poverty of the hovels"). It is about the islanders' heroes (Toussaint), their flora and fauna (para grass, *cacaoyers, sapotille, gheko, colibri, épervier, coryanthas, daturas*), and their festivals (Saint-Jean and its fair). It is about the symbolic use of the *lambi* (conch shells) as an instrument of revolt, an instrument to call the slaves to revolt during Toussaint's time. With equal symbolism, the *pirogue* (canoe) and *pagaie* (oar) emerge as major tropes. Says the poet,

> But before I should tackle the orchards of the
>   future
> grant that I merit them, girded by sea,
> give me my heart as I await the soil
> give me upon this sterile ocean –
> whose promise of a securing-sail nonetheless
>   caresses the hand –
> give me upon this infinitely varied ocean
> the obstinacy of the noble dugout
> give me its sea-going strength
>
> Behold it as it advances heaving and pitching on
> the pulverized
> wave
> behold it dancing the sacred dance before the haze
>   of the burg,
> behold it bellowing like a giddy lambi

behold the lambi galloping to the very indecision
  of the bluffs
and behold the oar over and over
forcing the water
like a powerful plow
the dugout rears beneath the assault of the water's
  blade, shimmies a second,
attempts to flee, but the rough caress
  of the oar diverts it
and then it digs down, a shudder runs over the
  spine of the wave
the sea objects and scolds
but the dugout slips, like a sled, over the sand.

give me the muscles of that dugout on the troubled
  sea
and the convincing joyfulness of the lambi bringing
  the gospel! . . .

(Pallister 1978, 73-74; ll. 191-214)

The *pirogue*–the response to the slave ship and the vehicle of the legitimate negritude voyage, the metaphor of vital journey–becomes the most powerful image of the book. (According to Emile Snyder, it exemplifies the African's ancestral ways of contact with his peoples, the interior navigation of negritude.)[15] Additionally, the *pagaie* is the instrument of the leader, who guides those on his ark (his *pirogue*) to safety and freedom; the *lambi* is his means of communication, even his poetic voice.

While the above passage uses an almost encoded negritude lexicon, its eruptive joy, energy, and power are reminiscent of Rimbaud, especially his "Le Bateau ivre."[16] Although scholars have rightfully identified the Rimbaldian paroxysms strewn throughout the *Cahier*, this does not prevent it from being exactly what André Ntonfo has called it: "an authentic negro outcry."[17] The explosion is native, volcanic. As Césaire says in his interview with Michel Benamou, "I am a Pelean. I am from the mountain, of the mountain; I come from Basse-Pointe, from Mount Pelée; I am an explosive type."[18] (One is nonetheless permitted to make an analogy not only with Rimbaud, as regards the *pirogue*, but also with the Ethiopian Kwegu spitting water on his newly carved canoe and uttering such exhortations as "cut the water like a crocodile" or "float like foam.")

The notion of Christianity that I mentioned in speaking of Rimbaud and Césaire and their attitude toward "Christian" colonizers is, however, a complex one in the *Cahier*. For while the hypocritical "Christian missionary-hangman" has introduced Christianity to the black man and then told the latter he must bear his sufferings without murmur, it is the black man who has been the true figure of Christ in his passion. Elaborations of these problems have been worked out by several critics of the *Cahier*, Beverley Ormerod among the most notable. Ormerod maintains that Christ and the Marxist leader are fused in this poem and that through the Christ figure the paradise that was lost (Edenic Africa) is regained. There is transcendence, apocalypse, eschatology, and revolution. One of Ormerod's theories is that Césaire takes on the role of Messiah in the *Cahier*, for Christ, like Césaire, identified with the poor and the oppressed. The crown of thorns – one of the instruments of Christ's passion – figures importantly in the *Cahier*. Thus the tree symbolizes not only a type of cross but also constancy, harmonious integration, ascent, and resurrection, becoming a part-Christian, part-African allusion. But Ormerod finds the same symbolism of the tree, associated with courage and tenacity (like the *pirogue*), in other Caribbean literature as well, for example, in Jacques Roumain's *Masters of the Dew* and in Simone Schwarz-Bart's *The Bridge of Beyond* (Ormerod, 108).

The passage in which the child sucking on his stick of sugarcane merges with the man with the rope around his neck is interwoven with the recollection of the crown of thorns. Evident here is the birth of Christ – in this instance born into slavery – interlocked with His bitter passion. The passage in which Césaire recalls the ironies in the celebration of Christmas on the island, with its "painful mixture of forced gaiety and gnawing fear,"[19] also has important bearing on the issue. Religion as expressed here does indeed touch the existential realities of the people. As A. James Arnold warns, religion has a physicality of which we should be aware in our discussions of this topos. We should avoid relating it to a form of ascetic Christian mysticism à la Meister Eckhardt. Rather, religion as lived by the black man is conceived to be a "humbler manner of companionship with God, of familiarity not on the divine plane like that of the mystic but on the terrestrial plane. In other words, whereas thought dehumanizes man, here it is God who submits to the limitations of space and time, who initiates himself into the life of the body, who takes his place in the world and truly enrolls himself in the midst of our humility" (Arnold, 30; quoting from Césaire in *Tropiques*).

The indictment of the colonial educational system in *Cahier d'un retour* is similar to that of "Christianity" as lived in a colonial milieu, based fundamentally on a slave economy and on what the poet views as a racist mentality. Just as the question of Christianity is woven into the poet's childhood recollections, so too is the implicit criticism of colonial education. Neither priest nor teacher could rouse the protagonist of this powerful poem from his lethargy when he was a child, he says. This lethargy is due in part to hunger, in part to boredom. For what did they attempt to do, he asks, if not to pound into this little black boy's head the Ten Commandments and the story of Queen Blanche of Castille (*Cahier*, 39) – that is, the white man's religion, the white man's history? One is reminded, further, of the statue of Josephine, overlooking the park in Fort-de-France, referenced early on in the poem. She looks down from her heights, oblivious to the island, as, one might suspect, the island is somewhat oblivious to her. This island is essentially harsh and isolated – its sparse topography offering only an occasional palm tree, rigid and hardened like its very seed – with ubiquitous *mornes* (hills) that the poet ties to the sufferings of its people (*Cahier*, 37).

It logically follows that the poem now has an opening for developing a long list of moral abuses and of diseases that afflict the island and its black inhabitants. This "state of being" is translated by abstract nouns. Corruption and drift are so great as to be institutionalized and personified. They are "stretched like hammocks" – like the hammocks in which the people themselves stretch, reduced to indolence, hopelessness, renunciation – and are "on parade." It is no small wonder that, in this environment, the poet makes an effort to regain the golden moments of joy and interconnectedness symbolized by the umbilical cord, by the bread and wine of Communion, a blood of true marriages. But that recollection of former joy brings about an acute awareness of the present misery and poverty in the hovels. The speaker recalls *notre maison* ("our house"), the kind of house *all* of us lived in, a house sitting on cement blocks, with its metal roof (*coiffure*), pine-joint ceilings, straw chairs, shiny cockroaches (*Cahier*, 43). He recalls the good and the bad of his past, of the Christmases celebrated in great ambivalence, for there were the pleasures of *boudin* (thin, fat, spicy, hot) with plenty to drink (strong coffee, anise, milk punch, rum). There was the parish church with its warm and convivial atmosphere.

To remember this is to recall refrains from the Mass. To recall this is also to remember interludes of fear–fear of volcano, flood, poverty. Yet the city, to which the poet now returns, keeps growing. In this flat city life is flattened, dreams aborted, the "river of life hopelessly torpid in its bed" (and we note again personification, here of life and the city, as with the use of the hammock). Finally, the poet, as if scanning with his memory's eye, fixes on his native home, rat-infested, permeated by a bad odor, crowded with his six brothers and sisters, presided over by a sick, mercurial father and a mother tirelessly pedaling on the old Singer to ward off starvation, their metal roof patched and at times leaking (*Cahier*, 51-53). Like a central, enduring core, the bed of the grandmother stands on kerosene cans; it has a kidskin cover, dried banana leaves, and a worn-down mattress. This is where their roots lie, where they came from (*Cahier*, 55).

And so these very personal recollections–reflective of Césaire's insistence on the concrete–are woven in and out of the poem's public concerns. Like rows of coconut palms, the refrains of the Mass come and go, as do the alternating patterns of the pronouns: first *je* and then *nous*–family, compatriots. Similarly, the time references are fused so that the protagonist–the storyteller, the *griot*–plunges in and out of time, with the long-ago, the not-so-long-ago, and the longer-ago-than-long-ago all interlocked. Such an approach suggests a number of things. It establishes that the island people, like all peoples, have a past, present, and future, that they are not ahistorical. It also intimates that here past and present are not essentially different–and may even suggest that the future will not have to be like either the past or present.

If the poem is an outcry against the condition of the author's people, and a disturbing ledger of the humiliations, lynchings, lapidations, and other sufferings of his race, it is also a call to arms, an announcement of good tidings ("la bonne nouvelle"), a declaration that the old negritude is but a cadaver now, and that he, as poet-prophet-politician, holds his island by the hand as they stand erect against this tide of discrimination and deprivation, intent on change. Gone is the legacy of slavery and servitude that was the birthright of the blacks; gone are the doctrines of white supremacy that left even the blacks questioning themselves. There is work to be done: "It is not true," he says, "that the work of man is completed; . . . the work of man has only just begun, . . . and no race possesses a monopoly on beauty, intelligence, strength" (Pallister 1978, 75). The poet completely accepts his race, however worn and ravaged (*Cahier*, 128), to prepare for the apotheosis, says Snyder (1970, 210). The poet and his compatriots will go into the twentieth century as a creative force to be reckoned with, and their contribution will include the rejection of European rationalism and all its ills as they strongly maintain the existence of sources of knowledge more reliable than the intellect.

Earlier in the poem Césaire says, "Je vous hais, vous et votre raison" (*Cahier*, 73; "I hate you, you and your reason"), which should not be construed as a purely racist statement. Frutkin overstates the case when she writes, "His angry diatribes against Europe and the entire world are vivid testimony to what can only be described as anti-white racism, . . . an aggressive, violent, angry, if negative, racism" (Frutkin, 19). We have seen what Césaire means by this anti-rationalist stance. What we have not yet seen, however, is that in this poem Césaire prays that he be a lover of all men, or, to be more exact, that he not be a man of hate, for, as he explains, he hates the man of hate. He also points out that he fights the good fight to make his own race free, not because he hates other races. My translation of this passage clarifies the poet's exact position:

> make of me a man of endings
> make of me a man of new beginnings
> make of me a man of recollection
> but make of me also a man who can scatter seed
>
> make of me the one who executes these high deeds
> behold the time has come to gird up my loins like a
>   hero
>
> But in doing these deeds, my heart, preserve me
>   from all hate
> do not make out of me that man of hate
> for whom I have only hate
> for though I restrict myself to this race, the only
>   one of its kind,
> you know even so my tyrannical love

you know it is not out of hate for the other races
that I demand of myself that I be the prosecutor
    for this race,
    the only one of its kind,
that for the sake of universal hunger
for the sake of universal thirst
I want to call this race forth free at last
to produce from out of its walled intimacy
the succulence of fruits.

(Pallister 1978, 72-73, ll. 170-86)

Césaire believes that blacks must avoid imitating the errors of whites, especially their mistake of worshiping at the altar of science, technology, "progress," and loveless, sterile rationalism.

We have previously discussed this rejection of the rational approach to life that overlooks the important role of love. We have seen, moreover, that, as Césaire the poet would explain it, antirationalism is equally an aesthetic stance. He says in an interview that reason is rejected as a source of poetry in favor of the surrealist approach, which seeks poetry and perhaps even the answers to some of life's mysteries, beyond reality, in the realm of analogy and in the subconscious world of dream, nightmare, and hallucination (Benamou, 5). While the approach has something to do with the surrealist movement, and while Césaire can be classed among the modernists (see Arnold, 21-70), the antirationalist approach is nonetheless akin to the visionary quest of Rimbaud and *his* effort to see beyond the surfaces of things. The *Cahier* is not won over to surrealism's otherworldliness. On the contrary, the poem is firmly planted in the realities of this world, especially those of the Third World. The realities of poverty and illness abound: early in the poem we see an Antilles in which the sociogeographical setting is intertwined. With its frail inlets, muddy bays, damaging winds, and devastating volcanoes, the Antilles sees much of alcoholism, hunger, disease, martyrdom, and poverty, as well as smiles that only seek to cover up these ills.

Certainly this scene – followed by one in which the city (it must be Fort-de-France, for Josephine is "high above the 'négraille' ") gives us a no less foreboding picture – is no picture postcard, no tourist's paradise. The poet's return will not be built on nostalgia, and there are, according to Breton, even assaults on that potential nostalgia, for the natural splendor of the island is subverted by the human poverty, the exploitation, the vestiges of slavery. This return will be based on the drum roll we hear in the sixfold repetition of "au bout du petit matin" – at the end of the long night's absence, at the edge of childhood, after the creation of the child, after the birth of the poet. This is the moment when he returns, as if out of some unspoken but irresistible duty finally recognized and assumed. Grim reality is everywhere. Césaire has used surrealist techniques to compose this poem but above all to explore and define negritude. (Ironically, Keith Tribble explains that in the Soviet Union, where Césaire is viewed as a surrealist poet, or as a proponent of surrealist modernism, his poetry – although revolutionary – is thought to have nothing realistic enough for the proletariat [71]. Tribble claims that this is the dominant critical view of Césaire in the Soviet Union.)

Of course, the *Cahier*, with its wave of words and metaphors, which can only be called a spilling, like lava, is surrealist by the literary revolt it represents, not to mention the other types of servitude it repudiates, namely Western rationalism. It is a child of the surrealist movement and is certainly influenced by Breton, as Césaire's other poetic works would be. (Incidentally, according to Max Dorsinville, French Canadian surrealists and automatists, who were united in a movement called Refus global, identified with that spirit of revolt in Breton. Their thirst for political, artistic, and linguistic liberation was akin to Breton's and Césaire's. *Christophe*, in fact, was presented in Montreal at Expo 1967, not long after its composition.)

The matter of fertility brings up the question of the gender roles in this new departure. Like many other critics, Gérard Georges Pigeon suggests potential misogyny in Césaire, contending that the woman plays a secondary role in his works. In response to this Césaire says that the poem is, after all, epic, and that the so-called secondary role of woman is not a negative one. The woman of the Antilles, he suggests, represents earth and fecundity; it is she who "carries." The verb obviously has multiple meanings: she carries the children but is also the one who has maintained the race and its traditions, making the sacrifices required of the "porter." (To elaborate, the porter does not have his/her hands free for other action. Similarly, Zora Neale Hurston has characterized the black woman as the pack-mule of the race.) "The vegetable (woman) is the back-drop or staging, over and against which action is performed, by the animal"

(Pigeon, 5), says Césaire. (One sees in all this a somewhat floating concept of the vegetal, however, because, as in *Une saison au Congo*, the vegetable becomes the ideal state, to which the hero, Lumumba, "reverts.")

The accusation of misogyny in Césaire is in and of itself without much basis. It is true that some of the imagery can be jarring, as exemplified by "calmer than the face of a woman when she lies" (*Cahier*, 29). Still, while the male is clearly the agent of fecundation – "et toi veuille astre de ton lumineux fondement tirer lémurien / du sperme insondable de l'homme la forme non osée" (*Cahier*, 114-15; "and you, O star, from your luminous bed try to extract lemuridae / from the fathomless sperm of man; the as yet undared form" [Pallister 1978, 70]) – and while that fecundation is interlocked with the affirmation of negritude – "[Ma négritude] plonge dans la chair rouge du sol" (*Cahier*, 116-17; "it thrusts into the red flesh of the soil" [Pallister, 70]) – that fecundation would obviously be without issue if it were not accomplished on fertile land, with the receptivity of the female playing its role.

The accusation of the poem's misogyny is further unjustified when we consider the very important – indeed, central – section describing not only the mother at her Singer sewing machine but also the bed of the grandmother (*Cahier*, 55), who is to be construed archetypally as the mother of the race. The grandmother is pictured as the one who most drove home to the poet the need to read. (It might be fair to say that Césaire is essentialist, rather than misogynist.)

Primarily, the poet is affirming the masculine and feminine components of his sensibility, the dual nature of poet and politician, of reflection and action. Graziano Benelli, in his Marxist analysis of the *Cahier*, which he labels the "Cahier de la négritude," finds that negritude, a weapon forged in the very midst of the struggle, has two aspects.[20] One is poetic (the search for an authentic means of expression), the other is political (the concrete liberation of the masses). These poles are constantly being weighed against one another in *Cahier*, but this does not negate Benelli's assertion that Césaire's is a militant and revolutionary negritude, more so than Senghor's, whose negritude he calls "equivocal." In the *Discours sur le colonialisme*, Césaire's negritude becomes even more Marxist, according to Benelli; there Césaire will insist on the necessity of a materialistic negritude.

This dual nature, however, is also fed by the double cultural influences – the European (learned, borrowed, or, more accurately, imposed) and the African (the authentic). Césaire's use of French cannot be put into the same category as the way Senghor or Bernard Dadié, French subjects of Africa, use it. It is altogether different. Césaire and Damas have French as their only language except Creole (which, moreover, he barely knows, according to Lilyan Kesteloot and Daniel Racine,[21] but some influences of which he might nonetheless reflect), and the assimilation of the French language along with the French culture was a fait accompli of the Antilles centuries ago. In Césaire's case the total acquisition of the language would have been fundamental to his colonial, assimilationist-type education in the Antilles. Still, Corzani makes a considerable point of studying Césaire's use of French as exceptional and as related to his race. Césaire thrusts one word at another, one syllable against another, says Corzani (194); he uses words that are unusual and erratic, that kill and give birth. Corzani (195-96) claims that Césaire's French writing is different from, not better than, the French writing of whites – different in essence, not in quality. Césaire's language "negrifies" and "animates" the landscape, and the survival of animism in his treatment of nature is characteristic of the view of nature found in the Antilles. Césaire's many images, like those found in other black poetry, are explained by this animistic past, says Corzani (215-17). We might even make a special bestiary of the *Cabier*, as has been done for *Une saison au Congo*, and include in it Pigeon's findings that the serpent stands loosely for both Martinique and Africa; that the horse is a vehicle of energy, poetic inspiration, strength, and freedom; and the hawk represents freedom and nobility. In any case, the poem's imagery and structure combine to present an outpouring that approaches stream of consciousness while managing to level traditional values and examine modern technological society. All this and more comes together to make the *Cabier* a modernist text, one of the classic poems of the twentieth century.

Structurally speaking, however, the poem is anything but amorphous. As mentioned, "au bout du petit matin" is repeated six times like a drum roll early in the poem. Later the phrase comes five times as the poet speaks of the inert city, of the desolate, unfed, sick, and hungry crowd, untouched by surrounding events. Five times in five paragraphs the crowd is said to be in fear. Five paragraphs on the *mornes* follow; in the fourth paragraph the word *morne* is repeated five times. This is indeed a startling and highly rhetorical way to open this long poem.

After the overture we have the recollections, often contrasting, of the sordid wretchedness of the interlocutor's past. Next comes a departure: the poet will go to Europe but then return, for he has the plan to be a part of the grand scheme, to be a man of the world and certainly not the representative of this little island, of which he is, to a considerable degree, ashamed. Not yet committed, and yet with an agenda, he is thought to be the representative of persecuted man the world over: "je serais, je retrouverais" – the conditional tenses flow from his pen as he describes his grandiose plans. (Here Scharfman [37] sees an identification with Christ.) Certain recollections and reclamations follow. Two-thirds of the way through the poem comes the passage that proves the turning point in the poet's life, the moment when true *engagement* must come forth. This passage is "confessional" to say the least. It is also one of the most oft-cited:

> But you must know how far my cowardice went.
> One evening in the streetcar, a Negro, across from me.
> A Negro as big as a pongo, who was trying to make himself small on a streetcar bench. He was trying to disown his gigantic legs and trembling hands – those of a starving boxer – on that filthy bench. And everything had left him, was leaving him: his nose which seemed like a peninsula adrift, his very Negritude which paled under the action of a tireless taw. And the tawer was Poverty. A fat lop-eared bat sprang forth and its claw strokes had become scars – scabby islets on his face. Or rather Poverty was a tireless worker, laboring over some hideous cartouche . . .
> He was a sprawling Negro without rhythm or shape.
> A Negro whose eyes rolled, bloodshot, bespeaking his weariness. . . .
> Poverty had taken unspeakably great pains to bring him to "completion" . . .
> . . . A comical, ugly Negro, and the women behind me chuckled as they looked at him.
> He was COMICAL AND UGLY.
> COMICAL AND UGLY, for sure,
> And I mustered forth a big complicitous smile . . .
> My cowardice was restored!
> I salute the three centuries which support my civic rights and
>   my minimized blood . . .
> my heroism; what a farce!

> I am cut out for this city, and it for me. . . .
>
> *(Cahier,* 101-5; my translation)

The poet's crime – the crime of his race – is to have seen things through the eyes of others (of whites, of those two apparently white women) and not to have seen himself (themselves) in that pathetic creature undermined by a personified Misère. Incidentally, in the above passage Poverty is called a "tawer" (a de-Negrofier, a force that whitens the skin as well as the soul, just as the tawer whitens leather). The negative charge of the word *white* in the Toussaint passage is thus reinforced here as elsewhere in the poem.

But from this point on, the poet, realizing that he has been a traitor to the truly poor and downtrodden of his race, undergoes a conversion and becomes the "cannibal" he should always have been. He declares that he is completely involved in the struggle for equality and freedom, that his race stands now erect, the old negritude of subservience and complicity now dead. He reclaims all that makes up his negritude and repudiates the swamp and the shackles. He predicts the downfall of the arrogant white race and calls for undivided fraternity: "The dove of peace must now prevail, the total embrace, the kiss" *(Cahier,* 147-55). Like most negritude poems, this poem rises from the depths of despair and anger over the lot of the race, to reach new heights, with the newfound strength and courage coming through reaffirmation and rediscovery.

The movement at the end of the *Cahier* is an ecstatic, upward one – triumphant, apocalyptic, eschatological. Here the poet abandons his dark vision for a life of creativity, adjuring the "dove" to "climb, climb, climb" and declaring that he follows that dove. This vision is unforgettable, stamped on his cornea. In the dark hole in the sky where he had formerly wished to drown himself he now wishes to fish for (or out) "the malevolent tongue of the night in its unmoving *'verrition'" (Cahier,* 155). This *verrition* seems to be both a process by which light is prevented from spreading – is trapped or confined – and, according to Césaire, a scanning motion, a neologism constructed from the Latin verb *verri* ("to sweep," "to scrape a surface," "to scan"). Snyder renders this word *verrition* by the English word *flick*. (See James Clifford, where the last line is envisioned as an example of imagistic compression.[22] See also Clayton Eshleman and Annette Smith's translation as "veerition," a neologism reflecting the English verb *veer* [*CP*, 26].) In the darkness of prejudice and racial hatred the poet intends to find poems of self-celebration, celebration, and refutation – poems that carry forth the revolution undertaken when the poet recognized he was going down the wrong path, was goring his own ox. The final two words carry out, of course, the duality so often seen in the poem, for a "motionless veering" is, among other things, a powerful oxymoron. It is little wonder that Clifford should say, "Césaire does not restore the 'meanings' of language, culture, and identity; he gives them a turn" (Clifford, 177).

What is especially striking, we must conclude, is the powerful assertion of racial dignity and the insistence on equality among all humans that Césaire articulates in his final lines:

> And we are erect now, my country and I, our hair blown by the wind, my hand small now in its enormous fist, and strength is not in us but above us in a voice which pierces the night and all listeners like the arrival of an apocalyptic wasp. And the voice announces that Europe for centuries has stuffed us with lies and swollen us with pestilence,
>
> for it is not true that the work of man is
>   completed,
> that we have nothing to give to the world,
> that we are the parasites of the world,
> that it is enough that we should get in step with the world
> but the work of man has only just begun
> and man still has to conquer every forbidden thing
>   immobilized in the corners of his fervor
> and no race possesses a monopoly on beauty, intelligence,
>   strength,
> and there is room for everyone at the meeting
>   point of conquest, and we now know that the
>   sun revolves around our earth, lighting the
>   parcel which our will alone has engaged, and
>   that any star falls from heaven to earth at our
>   limitless command . . .
>
>   (Pallister 1978, 75; ll. 226-46)

The *Cahier* is an ethically bound text, and our analysis may remain a purely ethical one, without doing violence to it or to ourselves. In doing so, however, we should note that, just as Janheiz Jahn claims in his *Muntu*, the negritude poem represents a radical departure from the poetics of surrealism by its strong intention to dominate the word, and we are therefore dealing with a poem that has function and meaning behind its artistry, which goes beyond the goals of most surrealist poets of the Continent.

One of the ethical questions raised concerns the poem's medium of expression. Were we to look at Jean-Paul Sartre's discussion in "Orphée noir" of the use of French by negritude poets, we would come away with the notion that it is almost another language, that other linguistic and rhythmic systems have been superimposed on its genius, that, moreover, the poet uses the language of the oppressor and hurls it back in his face.[23] This is to some extent true of Césaire, but he, unlike many African poets, has claimed the French language as his by virtue of history; he really has no other. He is eminently a poet of the French language in the same way Rimbaud and Saint-John Perse are, and his use of the language tells us as much about his poetic genius as it does about his black origins, if not more. Assuming we could separate the two, it is not so much the use of the language as the paean to negritude (to which the language is the servant) that impresses us. That is why Ormerod can contend that the *Cahier* has set up the agenda for the whole of Caribbean literature, for its themes and aims (Ormerod, 2-11).

It might, however, be worthwhile to examine to what extent an ancient myth of the Caribbean area can be touching Césaire. There are curious parallels between passages of the *Cahier* and the sacred lyricism of the Nahuatl and the ritual songs of the Chiripà-Guarini, especially in the invocation of the Colibri (loosely translated as a hummingbird) and of other peoples of Central and South America devoted to the serpent, especially the Maya. Caribbean peoples share these traditions – not always from Africa, perhaps. (Nicolàs Guillén, for example, has many poems in which incantations to or the charming of the snake occur. African or Caribbean?)[24]

Historically, negritude asserted the legitimacy of belonging to an African culture. The negritude movement's greatest achievement was that it allowed for a genuine African feeling for life and attitude toward life to be expressed in a European language. Negritude implies not only a reappropriation of the word but, more importantly, dominion over it. The negritude movement has – especially in its poetry – affinities with the surrealist movement by its declaration of irrationality as a virtue in the human species, by its desire to shock the bourgeoisie, and by its celebration of "primitivism" and revolution.

But this is a very complicated issue, and we should bear in mind that as far as Senghor is concerned, the African worldview has always been one that embraced the sur-real, the supra-real. For him the black poet needs not the European surrealist movement to call upon the intangible world of spirits and dreams.[25]

In Senghor's *Anthologie de la nouvelle poésie nègre et malgache* we find the basic themes and beliefs of the first generation of negritude poets, which included Césaire, of course, along with Paul Niger, Guy Tirolien, Bernard Dadié, Léopold Senghor, David Diop, and Léon Damas. (A second generation of negritude poets included René Depestre, Anthony Phelps, Lamine Diakhaté, Tchicaya U'Tam'si, and Edouard Maunick.) These themes included, as Collins says in her preface to *Black Poets in French*, "powerful pride in Blackness; sorrowful and bitter evocations of the horrendous history of slavery, searingly eloquent anti-colonialism; repudiation of assimilated white culture; the warmth, color and beauty of the African respect for life; and emphasis on the overwhelming capacity of the proud Black race to love, despite its suffering. . . . Negritude was essentially a revolt against the oppression of the Black race by the white race, fused with the desire to restore human dignity to the Black man who had borne four centuries of servitude" (Collins, xvii). In "Orphée noir" (collected in Senghor's anthology) Sartre had adumbrated the attributes of this movement when he spoke of this poetry as a clarion call to arms, a declaration of the New Gospel,[26] in which the passion and crucifixion of the black race is over. He maintains that the poets are not writing for whites but for their own race. I think he is wrong, that they are writing for both, but in any event Sartre correctly finds this poetry to be *engagé,* although he certainly overlooks the fact that all art is to be functional in the African aesthetic. It seems, too, that he contradicts himself when he suggests that this poetry is *poésie pure,* for how can it be both purely lyrical (or nothing but lyricism) and functional?[27]

If Césaire in the *Cahier* coined the word *negritude,* he later defined it as "the simple recognition of the fact of being black, the acceptance of this fact, of our black destiny, history and culture" (Collins, xvii). Senghor scarcely differs in his definition of negritude as the totality of black values, of black culture the world over; that is, "the sum total of the economic and political, intellectual and moral, artistic and social values, not only of the peoples of Black Africa, but also of the Black minorities of America, of Asia and Oceania."[28] As Senghor elaborates his theories in his poetry and philosophical works, however, we find that for him negritude is more conciliatory, more bent on "aggressive assimilation" – taking what you want from the white man's culture and rejecting the rest. Although negritude necessarily implies a call for change, one could safely say that Senghor's view is less revolutionary and Marxist than Césaire's.

Even though negritude poetry focuses on the sorrows and sufferings of blacks, it is not pessimistic. The negritude poem tends to open at the end, to look forward to a future that will, because of the envisaged revolution, bring with it revenge, perhaps, but certainly a better life. Meanwhile, the characteristic of the black will be to lie patiently in wait; his will be the long waiting, the long patience. As the revolution is being prepared, great leaders and "culture heroes" have and will come forth to guide the people to equality and freedom. The exemplum in *Cahier d'un retour au pays natal* is Toussaint Louverture; in *Ferrements* it is Louis Delgrès, the last defender of black liberty in Guadeloupe, killed in 1802; in *Moi, laminaire* it is Léon-Gontran Damas, Michel Angel Asturias, and Wilfredo Lam; in *La Tragédie du roi Christophe* it is the legendary Henri Christophe; and in *Une saison au Congo* it is Patrice Lumumba.[29]

With these heroes the poet assumes a spiritual communion with the dead.[30] Moreover, he reflects the universal mythos in which a savior arrives to extract sufferers from their wretched state but in the process becomes a scapegoat. The rescuer or enabler can be identified in many contemporary African-American novels, although the culture hero/rescuer/salvation figure/mentor/enabler theme is common to all cultures and folk mythologies. The figure is used in negritude literature partly to highlight the historicity of the black race, to celebrate and validate the race and its most illustrious members. Sometimes it is used to provide exempla, other times to pinpoint victimization. The culture hero is also incorporated into negritude literature to portray the scapegoat syndrome in a societal construct and to imbue martyrdom with deeper spirituality.

Aimé Césaire fashioned the word *negritude* after the negative word "Negro" and the noun suffix "-tude," thus removing it from the domain of other *-isms* and distinguishing it from the Spanish term *negrismo*, which implies quite another thing. As is evident in his interview with Lilyan Kesteloot, Césaire recognizes the extent to which the concept has been used and then abused: "It has tended to become a school, to become a church, to become a theory, an ideology. I am in favor of negritude seen as a literary phenomenon, and as a personal ethic, but I'm against building an ideology on negritude."[31] He goes on to say, "My conception of negritude is not biological, it is cultural and historical. I think there's always a certain danger in basing something on the black blood in our veins, the three drops of black blood" (Kesteloot and Kotchy 1973, 236).

The *Cahier* is a political poem, *engagé*, calling for a revolution based on anger, rage, and hatred for abuse that will function as the bad conscience of the white colonists. It is also profoundly lyrical, issuing from the bowels of the poet and from his identification with the sufferings of his people. Like tragic drama it has its Orphic descent into darkness and its ascent to light; it has its ecstasy and engaging effusions. Its lyricism is permeated with sensuality, with aromas, sounds, tastes, and sights of every kind – the good, as in the *boudins* at Christmastime, and the bad, as in the sight of whip wounds, like zebra stripes on a black man's back. These vivid sights inspired Maximilien Laroche to study the poem from a cinematographic perspective: "[Césaire's] discourse revolves around his subject like a moving camera on its tracks."[32] Laroche identifies passages that we might call fade-ins and fade-outs and speaks of the repetitions and the accumulations (which can be cinematic, but also aspects of the poet's incantatory discourse). But he fails to see the relationship between this poem, which he rightfully discerns to be dramatic and visual, and the collections of dramatic poems and the plays to follow.

Some later works will still partake of that peculiar brand of surrealism which is Césaire's own and which embraces the movement he founded. In all we will see the dispensation of Western reason; the evocation of ethnic history and the very inscription of ethnicity; the call to decolonization and revolution that is simultaneously social, political, and literary; and the enlistment of such stylistic devices as loosely conceived strophes, repetition, ellipses, condensation, antiphrasis, oxymoron, occasional parody, and, above all, irony. A. James Arnold goes as far as to call the *Cahier* "The Epic of Negritude," and one might indicate that, whether or not we agree, Arnold's choice of this tag at least goes to show the extent to which epic and lyrical modes are fused in this masterpiece.

This is the story of one man's maturation, his evolution from shame to pride, a common theme in African and African-American literature as observed in such works as Camara Laye's *L'Enfant noir*, Sembène Ousmane's *Les Bouts de bois de Dieu*, Elaine Hansberry's *Raisin in the Sun*, Toni Morrison's *Song of Solomon*, and Alice Walker's *The Color Purple*. It is also the story of the coming of age of the race: the dog stands up to the master and "bites the hand" it no longer wishes to be fed from. It is the first in a long line of works by Césaire dealing with anticolonialism, decolonization, rebellion, and revolt.

I must note that the premise of the negritude movement was the butt of considerable criticism by some later black writers. Wole Soyinka, for example, is known for his stinging remark that a tiger, after all, does not declare its "tigritude," thereby suggesting the artificiality of the movement. Some of the concepts of negritude have been questioned and criticized; for example, by the Martiniquais playwright Daniel Boukman, and by Maryse Condé, especially in her plays *La Mort d'Oluwémi d'Ajumako* and *Dieu nous l'a donné*. In her "Pourquoi la négritude? Négritude ou révolution?" of 1973 she analyzes the movement in what some have considered "specious arguments." Her reservations concerning negritude are also elaborated in a 1984 *Jeune afrique* interview with Ekanga Shungu. The position of Chiekh Hamidou Kane (author of the famous novel *L'Aventure ambiguë*, which poignantly portrays the African's "ambiguous" problem of reconciling Western time and values) has no doubt been one of the most clearly articulated: Kane calls for African literature to move beyond negritude, for "the flag of negritude was something that we had no choice but to raise at a certain given moment in our evolution . . . but the time must come when all that is related to negritude must be relinquished, unless we wish to become completely hidebound."[33] Kane feels that if negritude is not relinquished, it could become a new kind of imperialism dividing Africans from the rest of humanity.

And as late as 1988 the African Literature Association chose as one of the themes of its conference "Négritude: Passé or Relevant?" *Présence africaine*'s traditional role as the movement's organ was examined there also. Albert H. Berrian's responses to this *mise en question* in the Summer 1988 *ALA Bulletin* are useful for further exploration, although the materials found therein under the negritude rubric are by and large of a personal note and do not really deal with the issue critically. Yet whatever these writers and scholars conclude, few of today's black Francophone writers can say they owe no debt to the positions promulgated by the negritude poets, which have functioned as their point of departure or as a current against which to direct their own visions.

Chapter Two

The Poetry Collections

Les Armes miraculeuses

In 1944 Aimé Césaire published another collection of poetry, *Les Armes miraculeuses,* comprised of poems even more hermetic and more revolutionary than *Cahier d'un retour au pays natal.* Bertrand Visage asserts that with this collection Césaire's poetry becomes more complex, the poet now having found in surrealism – and in his friendship with André Breton – a stimulus to take more risks in associating of images.[1] These images, Visage claims, are more hazardous, but they are always sustained by the obsession of the tom-tom, the taste for rhythm, the mixture of verse and prose. The collection is marked, too, he says, by semantic ambiguity.[2]

The collection's very title showed that the "new negritude" had taken up its arms, its weapons, and that the struggle had at that point assumed a new tone of aggression and resistance. This recueil included the dramatic poem *Et les chiens se taisaient* (discussed in chapter 3), which Eshleman refers to as the coda of the collection (*CP,* 22). Like the recueils of the French Renaissance, this one contains interrelated poems and must therefore be taken as a whole. The titular poem is, incidentally, carefully examined from a structural point of view by John Erickson, who claims that it "valorizes the power of the word, or, more precisely, the revolutionary power of the poetic discourse."[3]

Person and persona are again problematic, as in *Cahier d'un retour au pays natal,* perhaps even more so. The author, the agent, seems absent. Who is speaking and in the name of whom? The themes of the island "prison," of the ills and oppression of colonialization, against which is pitted the theme of rebellion – coming in many forms, or having many weapons – again surface. These themes, expressed through surrealist (or, as some prefer, magic realist) and automatist techniques, include allusions to the German occupation of French territories as a type of any colonial "occupation," and they present the idea that poetry is the principal miraculous weapon. Poetry is "enlisted" in the negritude "cause" like a shield or coat of arms, sometimes impenetrable, but also like a spear or any weapon able to pierce colonialism and racism, the arch enemies. Moreover, the volume traces the mythic and heroic journey of the poet-narrator-warrior in his battle against the "elements."

As a meditation on poetry, this convulsive and militant collection opens with a warning, "Avis de tirs" ("Warning: shots will be fired" or "Warning: heavy artillery is to be shot off in the vicinity"). These shots, directed at many of the same ills targeted in the *Cahier*, truly delineate the tensions of the postwar era, with its occupations, power struggles, and disregard for the conditions of the down-and-out. The work also entails veiled references to the tensions inherent in the writing process. One of the most remarkable poems in the collection from this point of view is "Batouque," which uses the Luso-Brazilian name for black dances of Brazil as something of a "call to arms." Césaire repeats this word 30 times or more to establish a sort of rhythmical *mise en relief* that structures the poem and epitomizes the oppression suffered by the colonized Martiniquais. But that is not all, for as Aliko Songolo shows, the act of dancing this dance defies the established social order, and thus the word, and the dance, represent rebellion.[4] "Batouque" has been the object of many studies and commentaries: Songolo, of course, gives it ample space, but it is also examined by A. James Arnold (134) and Bernadette Cailler[5] and is the object of a comparison with Gaston Miron in an important article by Eloise Brière.[6] (Césaire returns to the Batuque [as he then spells it] in "Le verbe marronner, . . . à René Depestre," from the 1976 collection *Noria.*)

Gregson Davis has aptly said that *Les Armes miraculeuses* "refract[s] the harsh realities of life in a colonial outpost under the shadow of the Vichy government" (*NVC*, 5). But the collection is also obscure and hermetic, perhaps because there is an unresolved tension between its themes and the metaphoric-associative approaches used to express these themes. Clayton Eshleman and Annette Smith liken *Les Armes miraculeuses* to a "trampoline that resists penetration at the same time it affords an exhilarating 'ride'" (*CP*, 21). Despite this obscurity, however, a couple of the poems are accessible. "Perdition," like several poems in the collection, offers a prophesy, while the title poem "Les Armes miraculeuses" speaks to the ancestral cultural load that is to be recovered: the birds, says the speaker, will sing the Congolese lullaby that the "soudards" (ugly white colonial soldiers) have made him "unlearn." The poem asserts, then, the rich human activity that lies buried in prehistory and that must be taken into account.

"Le Grand Midi" ("High Noon") is easily the collection's most stunning poem. Césaire uses the *pirogue* motif of *Cahier d'un retour* and intertextually echoes Rimbaud, carefully rescribing the Frenchman's verse for his own purposes. Describing a feeling of incapacity and hesitation followed by decision and resolve, this poem is also a prereading of *Et les chiens se taisaient*. It seems to be Le Rebelle of *Et les chiens* who is saying out of a victimized agony:

> Qui fêle ma joie? Qui soupire vers le jour?
> Qui conspire sur la tour?
> Mon sang miaule
> des cloches tintent dans mes genoux . . .
>
> (Who cracks my joy? Who sighs toward light?
> Who conspires on the tower?
> My blood howls like a cat
> and bells clang in my knees . . .)[7]

But the persona of his poem (described as "Fragments") resolves not to wait. (Why wait?) Instead, in the closing movements he cries out, like the poet of *Cahier d'un retour*, "Arrière! je suis debout." It is time to act! Therefore, he says, "Je marcherai . . . je pars je pars . . . j'avance plus sûr et plus secret et plus terrible que l'étoile pourrissante" (*AM*, 59-60; "I shall march . . . I am on my way; I am on my way . . . I advance, more certain, more secret and more terrible than the rotting star"). "Le Grand Midi" can well be regarded as a bridge poem between *Cahier d'un retour* and *Et les chiens se taisaient*.

Soleil cou coupé

In 1948 Césaire published *Soleil cou coupé*, a title with an obvious debt to Apollinaire. Eric Sellin suggests that the image in this collection evokes the rising sun that has been cut off from the horizon.[8] Thomas Hale goes on to note that the images of the sun used here also flow from those in Rimbaud as well as in Paul Claudel, especially in his *Tête d'or* (Hale 1978, 13-16). Hale points out that it is not just the images but their impact on the universe that is at play here, for the imagery conveys the idea of seasonal cycles, of weather modifications, of the sun's metaphorical power as judge of mankind. Indeed, he contends, the sun is virtually deified; this solar god is associated with the poet's desire to return to his origins. Equally interesting is that in this collection, as Hale points out (291), the poet's earlier surrealist inclinations are somewhat less marked: the poems are less hermetic and more optimistic. (Can this optimism be linked to the political successes that Césaire was then experiencing, in which departmentalization was realized and seemed – at least momentarily – to promise a better standard of life for the Caribbean Francophone islands? Hale seems to think so.)

Soleil cou coupé originally contained the poem "A l'Afrique" ("To Africa"), which might point to the direction Césaire's poetry was to take. This poem first appeared (with one stanza that was ultimately suppressed) in 1946 in the journal *Poésie 46*; it reappeared with slight revisions in the 1971 revised edition of *Les Armes miraculeuses* as "Prophesy," a poem "in which a contemplative speaker bears witness to a surreal transformation of his Caribbean seascape" (Arnold, 213). The poem was again reprinted in *Cadastre*, with some "crude and vulgar blasphemy" (Arnold, 213) omitted. The important thing to collect from all this is that the revised texts of "A l'Afrique" demonstrate the extent to which Césaire ultimately abandoned a mythic model of human experience – an Africa of the heart. His revisions carefully restore to history what once had been mere myth (see Arnold, 217-19). But leaving aside the question of infinite revisions, which make the particular edition one selects of prime importance, the message of *Soleil cou coupé* is one of self-sacrifice and mutilation, themes well-illustrated in "Lynch I."

In "Le Coup de couteau du soleil dans le dos des villes surprises" we again have prophesy, preceded by three visions that, as

Arnold shows (194-204), have passages from Revelation and Saint Matthew as important intertexts. Arnold's analysis is flawed, however, by his comparing translations of Césaire's text to those of the King James version of the New Testament. A comparison of Césaire's original language with passages from the Catholic version of the Apocalypse in French would be more valid and every bit as revealing. Regardless, the reader is referred to this section in Arnold for a thorough study of the structure and meaning of this central poem, which may well be an index to Césaire's religious perspectives. Rejecting the God of the Christians, he shifts to a modernist version of the Earth Mother, the alchemical-surrealist woman, Omphale, a chthonic goddess or nocturnal giant, an archaic female divinity of the underworld (Arnold, 201). Into this are woven allusions to Vever, the mandala of voodoo, which is the very definition of religious syncretism. But as one may gather by a syncretic summation of various critical viewpoints (Arnold, Cailler, et al.) and from the text itself, the poem conveys the idea that the black heart of negritude replaces Christ, that Nommo replaces Logos, and that the sun as a natural force subverts the role of God as a supernatural agency in the life of man. This is an anti-Catholic poem, vividly illustrating the effect of personal creativity as it confronts the monoliths of colonial society, namely the Catholic church. Similar replacements occur in "Lynch I," where the lynched man replaces the crucified Christ.

Like *Cahier d'un retour* and especially *Les Armes miraculeuses*, *Soleil cou coupé* is the record of a spiritual journey, enlisting more intensely than the other two the support of African animism and a fully articulated system of metaphors, including the Cesairean "bestiary" often discussed by scholars. Like the other two the collection is an assertion of the primacy of poetry as the principal logos, as the sun that purifies as it undergoes transformation and transforms. The power of the word is evident in the tremendous language play apparent in the collection's title, *Soleil cou coupé*, and in the play of words in "Le Coup de couteau." By the interplay of these two titles we see that the sun is both a passive and an active force. These plays on language are hardly new to Césaire; a good example from *Les Armes miraculeuses* is found in "Jour et nuit," with the marvelous play of the words *terre* and *ver(s)*: "de terre de ver cherchent parmi terre et vers."

Corps perdu

The title poem of *Corps perdu* (1949) is not without its references to
the surrealist view of life and the human body as fragmented. Yet despite this scattering, the umbilicus – a central and unifying agent – is
quite present here, as it is in much African art. The idea of possible
unification through centrality and natural phenomena is not new to
Césaire: in "Le Coup de couteau" the primal woman is called, among
other things, Omphale. Janheitz Jahn finds "Corps perdu" concerned with and expressive of the Ntu philosophy, which involves
the total relationship of all things and beings (Jahn 1968a, 118-19).

Corps perdu refers not only to the scattered and mutilated race
but also and more specifically to the poet's body – Osiris-like, orphic.
And within this cluster of symbols we must include too the concept
of the tragic, sacrificial poet who labors, Hercules-like, as a representative of the people, the collectivity. (So here we would recall that
Omphale was also the name of the mistress who purchased Hercules
as a slave; but, while present in the original version, this European
resonance is excluded in *Cadastre.*) *Corps perdu* evokes the scattering of the race, the diaspora. Thus the island as a place of alienation and isolation recurs, but the island is also the place of restoration. The phoenix symbol seen in Césaire's previous work recurs in
this collection – and not without bearing on the restoration motif – specifically in "Dit d'errance" ("Song of Wandering").

As he had done in *Soleil cou coupé*, Césaire constructs more
open poetry in *Corps perdu*, but he also begins to question the concept of Africa as Paradise Lost, especially in "Dit d'errance," in which
the poet says he is bringing low the trees of paradise. Césaire adopts
the image of the volcano, which, as Hale points out, will become a
major metaphor in his poetry. Yet we should also note the important
poem "Ton portrait,"[9] which is reminiscent of Langston Hughes and
which vividly announces Christophe's apostrophe to the river in *La
Tragédie du roi Christophe.* No metaphor is more characteristic of
Césaire, except perhaps the escaped slave pursued by dogs, an image
we encountered in the *Cahier* and will again in *Et les chiens se taisaient.*

The most famous poem of *Corps perdu* is probably the first,
"Mot," often reprinted and commented on. Its power and violence
are uncommon, even for Césaire. In some respects it is the Césaire

poem most reminiscent of the slight style adopted by Damas, although the tone is certainly Césaire's. The "word" of the poem is *nègre* or *Negro*, which has a wide field of meanings that include hatred, pain, suffering, hangings. This word, like a spasm or hiccup, vibrates in the gullet, especially when pronounced in French. It is like the claw of the tiger, the shattering sound of bullets, or the tearing of taffeta. The lynchings and the poisoned arrows endured by the black ironically recall the Christian martyrdom of Saint Sebastian. But dualism is present here. If the word sounds ugly and stinging when lashed out by a white, it nonetheless is like a "roll of thunder in the summer" that comes from the liberties the blacks are now taking as their own, and as a matter of course. *Nigger* becomes *black*: both meanings are contained in the French word. The word *nègre* or *nigger* is like an exfoliating stigma, and, as Davis puts it (*NVC*, 118-19), the manner in which Césaire turns the negative word back on the user, making of it a sonorous challenge, reminds us of "Barbare" from *Soleil cou coupé*. The word *nègre* additionally functions to pinpoint the poet's relationship to words as they are read and spoken – verbal icons, to use an oxymoron. Within the context of this poem, which Arnold (226-27) compares to passages of Valéry's *Cimetière marin*, Césaire reiterates the theme of the poet-priest who must submit to the "vibrating arrow" and become the scapegoat of the community.

In his conclusion to a discussion of this collection, Arnold finds that *Corps perdu* as a title "has a profoundly ambiguous resonance" (250-51). And although Arnold finds many possible meanings for the expression, including the notion that the body must be lost in order to be reborn (as was certainly true in the myth of the phoenix – a privileged metaphor for Césaire, according to Kesteloot and Kotchy), he never once appears to relate the concept of the lost body to the myth of Orpheus, surely as pertinent as the Egyptian tale of Osiris, whose tragic fate Arnold recalls in his minute and statistical analysis. (It was clear, of course, in the original edition, that the "elle" in the "Dit d'errance" referred to Isis; it is therefore only by analogy that one should incorporate the story of Orpheus into the references to Osiris. The story of Orpheus is the story of Césaire.)

Ferrements

The year 1960 saw the publication of *Ferrements,* whose central image replaces the concept of armor as an iron or steel coat with that of the iron chains of slavery. The collection focuses on the future (*devenir*) rather than the present (*être*), however, and it again introduces the theme of the renaissance of the black race, symbolized by the phoenix. This collection communicates a message of hope to the oppressed through such metaphors of fertility as pollen and ripe fruit. The poems function in terms of antithetical or dialectical configurations, such as doubt versus certainty, servitude versus freedom, anguish versus hope. As with many of Césaire's works, this collection contains such classical allusions as the Promethean myth (in "Ferment"), which shows how the poet challenges the Sun, seen as an eagle devouring his liver. Perseus is invoked in "Me centuplant Persée": playing on the words *perce, transperce,* and *Persée,* the poet shows how perseverance and *attente* – important "arms" of the negritude program – ripen him for battle; the poet, like a tree, shows the rings of the years that have recorded all the "volcanoes."

The tree image, which becomes a full-blown metaphor in Césaire's plays, recurs here, as do the vampires or cannibals of the *Cahier*[10] and the dog imagery of the *Cahier* and *Et les chiens se taisaient* (*F,* 25). The primary tropes of the collection, however, are the roll of the seasons and the sense of *attente* and preparation.

Time is an essential subject of *Ferrements.* Whereas in *Cahier d'un retour* we may have felt time as a pressure – the poet and his people being in a hurry for change, for revolution – here time, conditioned by sun and moon, is viewed (especially in "Comptine") as a molding process, in which that *lente patience* which is an attribute of negritude brings the race to a sufficient state of ferocity. "Hors des jours étrangers" exhorts the race to come into its own, to evolve its "own head," to cease to be the toy at other men's carnivals, the scarecrow in their fields. The speaker encourages the people to overthrow their oppressors and disenfranchisers through their tears and their rage, which will be like a salubrious storm (*F,* 81). Ronnie Scharfman studies the spatio-temporal problems of this poem at length and appears to see it as a fitting example of Césaire's *poésie engagée* (96-101). "The whole ambition of this text," she writes, "aims at liberation through reversing the existing alienated order"

(Scharfman, 100). We cannot, strictly speaking, say that a "text" has "ambition," yet the poet does indeed marshal the Marxist ideology of leveling and fresh construction as liberating measures, just as Scharfman implies.

While the first half of *Ferrements*, as Hale (1978, 396-97) correctly observes, deals with slavery and the sad past of the race, the second half looks to future action. Hale judiciously notes that one not only finds all of Césaire's preferred images – island, volcano, birds, animals, trees, and the sun – but also "for the first time" a series of elegies consecrated to Louis Delgrès, Paul Eluard, Emmet Till, and the black labor leader Albert Cretinoir. Yet in a very real sense one might justifiably argue that the *Cahier* already contained such an elegy in memory of Toussaint Louverture. These elegiac poems tend to fall into the second half of the volume and are therefore apt to be allied with an optimism through a sense of leadership or at least of action not present in the first section. The brevity and highly accessible symbolism of the little African-style poem "Small Song for Crossing a Big River" do not diminish its effectiveness; rather, the little song, taken from the Yoruba, attenuates the optimism of the second half, for the ending speaks of the great palm trees' force as stifled by the huge burden (of the storm, or the wind).

Lilyan Kesteloot (in *AC*, 291-300) and A. James Arnold (252-82) have extensively commented on the poems of *Ferrements:* both see the collection as the result of a new poetics. Arnold, who recalls Kesteloot in his analysis, finds that the 48 poems display considerable stylistic diversity and that the collection as a whole has three voices. It in fact contains songs of combat and songs of praise, the latter reminding us somewhat of the African praise song in structure and especially in intent. Of these, the poems "Africa" and "Salute to Guinea" are notable: they can be said to express Césaire's praise at what he sees to be an end of colonialism in Africa, the arrival of the African nations at Hegelian wholeness and solidarity. Arnold (265) contends that in this collection the dialectical process of history is, for Césaire, more Hegelian than Marxist. (Césaire, however, might today view the so-called decolonized situation somewhat differently.) The reader would do well to examine Césaire's essay "The Political Thought of Sékou Touré" in conjunction with his poem "Salute to Guinea." The essay clarifies Touré's rejection of communism – as much as capitalism – as a Western *ideology* or philosophy; it shows how he willed a restitution of African and specifically Guinean values and social institutions in his decolonization program. Touré's rejection of Western rationalism and insistence on self-determination as a moral imperative and psychological necessity is in harmony with the goals of Césaire. This exposé of the Guinean leader, who is represented here as anything but the dictator Western circles perceive, portrays him as a man to be admired.

In other poems in this collection the topos of the mutilated hero is transferred to the suffering people. Arnold specifies that the collection sometimes manifests the Nietzschean notion of the redeemer hero, but a hero whose contribution is conditioned by the prerequisite that his sacrifice not be a purely social one: this is tied to the idea of the poet whose quest is at once poetic, spiritual, and, coincidentally, social. (Social because with the negritude poets we never encounter *l'art pour l'art* but always, as with such other art forms as sculpture, music, architectural appointments, and dance, a creation at once aesthetically pleasing and functional.)

Cadastre

Cadastre, containing two previously published recueils – *Soleil cou coupé* and *Corps perdu* – was published by Seuil in 1961. In his study of *Cadastre,* Jacques Chevrier finds that the collection, which delineates what he calls a painful combat or struggle, has no "schéma d'ensemble," no "dramatic progression." Rather, it is a nebulous gathering of themes and images that constitute "keys" the reader must patiently count and decode. We find metaphors pertaining to suffocation, struggle, and victory; we sense opacity, a fixation with imperfection or lack, while a decomposed Europe is depicted through imagery of petrification and rot. On occasion, says Chevrier, a corrective is added (Chevrier, 95-97). To Chevrier's charge that the volume lacks cohesion we might respond by noting that we are dealing here with two distinct volumes and that it was more Césaire's intention to "clean up" his early poems than to present a recueil in which the individual pieces relate to one another or present a singular dramatic thrust. His modifications of *Soleil cou coupé* in particular are extensive. Hale concludes that despite Césaire's apparent intention to minimize the excesses of surrealism in *Corps perdu* by modifying *Cadastre,* "the collection does not lose its Surrealist nature" (1978, 409-10).

From *Cadastre* comes one of Césaire's most famous poems, "Exvoto pour un naufrage." Kesteloot (in *AC,* 291-300) finds this poem one of the most transparent, one of the most thematically, lexically, and syntactically lucid. Although the poet sings in a style reminiscent of a *griot* or cult slave preceding the cortege of a black king, the piece contains a strong dose of that irony so characteristic of Césaire, for here the king is The White Man of South Africa. Use of the tom-tom again supplies the rhythms evoking the Black Man's word, so "enigmatic for foreigners." In the opening lines the white supervisor searches for diamonds that the miners may have cached in their mouths or anuses before leaving the mine, but then the poem moves through a highly condensed series of metaphors, alluding to the "three souls of the poet," at once the heart, brain, and liver as identified by the Caribbean Indian and also the three civilizations (i.e., Indian heart, European brain, and African liver). Especially striking are the allusions to the African culture hero Chaka, to the question mark of the scorpion (perhaps Africa, in mystical geography), and to the most famous "surrealist" image of all, "beau comme une machine à coudre sur une table d'opération" ("beautiful like a sewing machine on an operating table"), which perhaps harks back to the Singer of the poet's mother. After this comes a series of "flash" images that show the diminished power and greatness of the "king," no longer a healer who cures tuberculosis but instead one who gives it, he himself being sick, infected, and doomed to die. All here is dirisible, says the persona, who invites the reader-spectator to laugh. Kesteloot's detailed, sugestive analysis is excellent.

Noria

"Le verbe marronner," one of Césaire's most frequently cited poems, is found in *Noria,* which consists of previously published pieces. *Noria* first appeared in the *Oeuvres complètes* in 1976. "Le verbe marronner" is dedicated to the great Haitian poet René Depestre. One of the most important things Césaire is conveying here is that for him poetry must always be functional, must always be at the service of revolution. No matter how much people may not like it, he seems to be saying, "le fond conditionne la forme" ("the content of the poem dictates and conditions its form"). This position considerably distances Césaire from the continental Parnassian and symbolist poets' espousal of art for art's sake. It makes of Césaire not only a consummate surrealist–for the surrealists espoused the notion that art, while not being polemical, should serve revolution[11]–but also a true African in his aesthetics. Central to this poem is the play on the word *marronner* ("to maroon, to abandon, to give something a chestnut color"; to pull the chestnut out of the fire, and alluding also to the fugitive slave). Derived from American Spanish *cimarrón* (wild, unruly) and from the Old Spanish *cimarra* (thicket), the word has been fused with the French word *marron*, derived from Italian *Marrone* (a chestnut color), to create multiple associations and meanings. (The verb form is similarly used in the *Cahier:* "mon audace marronne.")

Moi, laminaire

In the preface to his most recent poetry collection, *Moi, laminaire* (1982; translated roughly as *I, ever-present, ever-entwining sea tangle*), Césaire tries to bring together familiar but irreconcilable realities, which might include time and nontime, past and future, north and south, east and west, life and death, fervor and lucidity, sun and shadow, mountain and mangrove, the sound of body and the halt. Using such polarities as a vehicle for poetic expression is hardly new to Césaire, nor is it original, although Bernadette Cailler[12] fixes on "Crevasses" ("Fissures"), intending to show these opposites as a source of tension, both poetic and political, because they are not to be resolved and therefore result in a vicious circle, a situation with no exit. In "Crevasses," she writes, "it seems that the nadir of the place of reverie has been privileged in this collection, as if it were a point that is closer to survival than to resurrection, closer to the fleeing moment than to eternity, a marginal-point, a lagoon-like retreat where a constellation of terms moves about exploring the efficacy of the hollow, of the wound, of the scratch, of the tooth-bite" (Cailler, in *AC*, 98; my translation). She seems to find the same phenomena at work in both "Calendrier lagunaire" and "Ça, le creux." "Crevasses" portrays that vicious circle of which I just spoke, the circle being an entanglement of sorts that leaves the narrator, after

300 years of climbing, not only still not at the top of the hill but confronted by fissures into which he might or must fall. Some consider the circle "non-vicious" (Davis, in *NVC*, after Césaire himself), but I think it likely that Césaire is working as he often does with dialectical rather than antithetical constructions. Imagistically, the cameleon-hornbill cluster suggests the basic but dialectical conflict between order and chaos: both are constant, neither will win. Cailler's analysis is very complex and somewhat hazy as she seeks to translate the images of the serpent, vine, and bird of prey, as well as what she calls "unidentified" insects that sting a "non-identified" narrator into everyday meanings. (The sting of the insects reminds us of Antoine Bolamba, who calls them good because they sting but do not suck the blood, as would a white colonist.)[13] The best part of Cailler's short piece about "Crevasses" comes toward the end, when she suggests that Césaire is communicating the notion that the epic grandeur of his own past, like the past of the race, is not present in these texts (i.e., there is no longer the possibility of a poetic ego or of such a leader as Toussaint or Le Rebelle).

The major metaphors and themes of Césaire's poetry collections are commitment, decolonization, and revolution, and all seek to liberate the individual, the race, and poetic creativity. Césaire announced many of these themes and metaphors in the *Cahier* and was to take them up as part of his permanent literary baggage in his plays, the first of which was *Et les chiens se taisaient.*

Chapter Three

Et les chiens se taisaient

The long lyric poem *Et les chiens se taisaient,* which appeared in 1944, is radically different from *Cahier d'un retour au pays natal* in that it partakes of drama and is, as Barthélemy Kotchy has labeled, a "lyric tragedy" (Kesteloot and Kotchy 1973, 129). A sustained revolutionary cry, this work announced the nature of Césaire's three subsequent plays. *Et les chiens* is a protest against the inhumanity of the colonial situation, which, to a considerable extent, is the political and social message of all the writer's drama. Césaire, in fact, sees the theater as better suited than poetry for the presentation of a social message. He endorses an aesthetic of the theater that is at once black-African and classical: the play is to divert and to instruct (Kesteloot and Kotchy 1973, 131, 135). Although all four of Césaire's plays are committed to the cause of showing the condition of the colonized black (often in a historical context), they focus effectively on different aspects of that colonization. Thus the time frame and locus vary from play to play while the fundamental impetus remains somewhat constant.

Et les chiens se taisaient, first published as a part of *Les Armes miraculeuses,* was revised and published as an *"arrangement théâtral"* in 1956.[1] It is indeed a "lyric tragedy," in which the colonized blacks' cries of protest and revolt are symbolized by the barking of dogs. But by a *dédoublement* of the symbolism, these barkings may also be those of the white man's watchdogs. One leg of the symbolism is strongly reminiscent of the famous sonnet of the Jamaican-born American poet Claude McKay:

> If we must die, let it not be like hogs
> Hunted and penned in an inglorious spot,
> While round us bark the mad and hungry dogs,
> Making their mock at our accursed lot.
> . . . .

Like men we'll face the murderous, cowardly pack,
Pressed to the wall, dying, but fighting back![2]

The work retains the character of a dramatic poem partly by its style. It is highly rhetorical, repetitive, and rhythmical – the rhythm suggested by repressed punctuation; repeated words, characteristic of Martiniquais speech patterns (i.e., *beaucoup beaucoup*); and rendering, via dialogue, of Caribbean cadences. It is also more poem than play because the speakers remain undifferentiated symbols. The main character, the hero, is called simply Le Rebelle, while other speakers are equally allegorical or symbolic: L'Echo, Le Choeur, Le Récitant, L'Amante, Les Folles, La Mère, Le Geôlier, and so forth. Yet in 1956 *Et les chiens se taisaient* was divided into three acts, like the three subsequent plays of Césaire. Moreover, the funereal atmosphere, the role of destiny, and the use of the chorus and L'Echo are all reminiscent of Greek tragedy and of Nietzsche's notions of Greek tragedy – debts Césaire has acknowledged (Kesteloot and Kotchy 1973, 139). Indeed, Nietzsche's central concept of the hero's voluntary sacrifice for the collectivity (promulgated in his *Birth of Tragedy*) foreshadows the engaged hero of existential literature and certainly greatly influenced the fashioning of Le Rebelle.

Césaire's use of the chorus, although certainly linked to Greek tragedy, is closely associated with certain other of his dramatic strategies to provide prophesy or commentary on the action, often from a societal viewpoint. In *Une saison au Congo*, for instance, the *joueur de Sanza* functions at once like a Greek chorus and an African *griot*. Moreover, though we may not compare the foreboding dreams of Pauline to the Greek chorus, surely the radio announcing his destitution to Lumumba has such a function, even if it is a modern device quite alien to the moralizing force of the Greek chorus. Un-Greek, too, is the humble status of our hero. Like Christophe, Le Rebelle is a slave; also like Christophe he is inhabited by "a royal being, asleep on a narrow bed" (*AM*, 126).

In the first speech of this "play" we learn, through exposition provided by L'Echo, that Le Rebelle is going to die and will not be widely mourned. His destiny is written in the sand; its architect is the arrogant white man (Orcus), who himself should "beware." The action is not by coincidence located on an island. Martinique and Jamaica are specified (*AM*, 127), but this could well be Saint-Domingue in Haiti. As we have seen, the island is a locus of imprisonment; here, as in the *Cahier*, the symbol is prolonged by Le Rebelle's prison cell being used as the setting for the poem's opening and closing scenes. Similarly, Le Rebelle could be Toussaint or Christophe, who knows similar solitude in life and is, like Le Rebelle,"Le Roi debout" in death. Le Rebelle is overcome by desolation at the start. He speaks with La Récitante. The sun (the lion) is about to come up. Its role in the salvation of the race is clear, but we are told that, in the beginning, before the sun, there was night: "Night and misery, comrades, misery, and animal acceptation; night rustling with slaves expanding beneath the christophorous steps, the great sea of misery, the great sea of black blood, the great wave of sugar cane and of dividends, the great ocean of horror and of desolation" (*AM*, 86). Therefore, as retribution for the whites' enslavement and exploitation of blacks and for their missionary zeal, the call to arms is "Death to the whites." All the speakers recognize the need for a leader – one who will hold a serpent in his right hand and a mint leaf in his left. On his head will be a dog's head, his sandals will be of pale sun. Finally, this lord, this king, arrives, announced by La Récitante, and it is Le Rebelle, "Le Roi debout," whom the others also proclaim. He claims that the flowers spring up at his passage: "I had led this country to a knowledge of itself; familiarized this land with its secret demons . . . and now [I am] alone . . . all is lonely" (*AM*, 93).

In the 1956 dramatic version of this poem, act 2 comes at this point,[3] and this movement of the work focuses on the leader's solitude. One tends to associate this doctrine of the lonely, misunderstood, unappreciated man of genius with the romantics, with such poets as Alfred de Vigny and Victor Hugo. It is a concept Césaire will rework in *Christophe* and in *Une saison au Congo*. But here the terms are highly poetic, and the speech of Le Rebelle is riddled with anguish and suffering. He speaks chiefly with La Mère and L'Amante. As will be the case for Mme Christophe, the women advocate compromise with the representatives of authority, Les Evêques, L'Administrateur, Le Geôlier, Le Messager. But Le Rebelle is intransigent. Despite his sense of isolation, his torment, and his fear of the flashes of past scenes that now appear before him (strings of cadavers, memories of slavery, brandishings, sadism of the master with his eyes of steel blue, death rattle of slave after slave) he will not give in, "not yet, not yet; I will return only in seriousness; love will shine in our burnt-barn eyes" (*AM*, 99). He has little to say to his mother, for she is of the setting sun, the past. Now the moment is red, the sun is rising. Le Rebelle has met Liberty, Freedom, a virgin girl who has been violated and is bleeding, a "ramp upon which mastiffs rage drunk" (*AM*, 101), and he must rescue her from indignities, injustices, and dangers. For there are, in fact, many kinds of dogs: faithful dogs that follow, serve, and protect their masters (the whites); police dogs that assist the lawmen in pursuit of the escaped slave; and the packs of wild dogs wandering through the cities and over the *mornes*. (The complexity of this dog imagery, which functions dialectically, is overlooked by Walker [116-18] and Kesteloot,[4] where the dogs are viewed only univocally as symbols of the "blancs oppresseurs.")

In these scenes Le Rebelle vividly recalls Christ,[5] scapegoat and savior, resolute in his intention to drive out the corrupt, interacting with his poor mother who pleads with him to save himself – soon she will be the Stabat Mater, ultimately the Pietà. But this mother is also the black mother, wellspring of sorrow for lost children (lynched, stolen, enslaved, murdered). She is harbor and recipient, the mule who carries on her back her laboring, beleaguered race, as Zora Neale Hurston has put it.

While Le Rebelle sees in the revolution he is mounting redress of past wrongs and a future full of sun, brightly colored parrots, fruit, fresh water, and breadfruit, his mother sees a desert that promises the whites' persistence in wrong and death for blacks. As spokeswoman for Césaire's humanism, the mother declares her race to be the human race, her religion to be fraternity. (Who says woman plays a subservient role in Césaire's work?) Her son is more cynical and vindictive, more modern and macho. He is more intent on continuing the revolt begun in the murder of his master; otherwise his son will be victimized. Thus his fraternity is larger than the mother's, more allied to Marxism. Le Rebelle will persist, though he will be, like Christophe, "un roi debout, qui ne possède rien" ("a king erect and dispossessed"; *AM*, 109), drawn off by the coursers of the night.

In liberating himself Le Rebelle also eliminates his brothers, but the people, made stupid by centuries of subjugation, do not follow their leader into freedom. Rather, in the third movement of the poem Le Rebelle is delivered into prison and unto death, thanks to the actions of his own people. They do not comprehend his vision. And so, as he undergoes a moment of fear and weakness (*AM*, 113), they deliver him over to the *békés*, the white colonial forces. Once in prison he rebels against his jailers, who ridicule and scorn him, as will happen to Lumumba in *Une saison au Congo*. He recalls again the horrors of slavery; he undergoes his Agony in the Garden (Kesteloot and Kotchy 1973, 143). Betrayed and sold, he realizes he speaks to deaf ears. He dies alone but not hopeless.

Obviously, this tragedy resides in the irony of the situation. The dog bites the hand that feeds it in several different ways. Tragic though the death of Le Rebelle is, like Christ's being chosen by the crowd to die in lieu of Barabbas, it is beneficial to all mankind, as the death of Lumumba will be. The road to freedom is not easily returned to wilderness. The inherent social, personal, and political tragedies depicted through the three movements are mitigated by this important gain. The revolt of the faithful dogs has been silenced, but the barking of the guard dogs is silenced too; all is at bay. Bane and boon are fused. With the title set in the imperfect tense, however, we understand that the faithful underdogs are silenced only temporarily. There will be more revolts: more leaders will rise against new masters; more dogs will appear on either side, barking at each other's heels. Who is to say, then, if one day it might not all be over? Where the imperfect exists, *passé défini* (completed past) is implicitly possible. (The symbolism of the dogs is discussed by Césaire in the Pigeon interview [5]. He points out there that the dogs have precedents in the jackal Anubis[6] of Egyptian mythology. Césaire effectively uses Anubis's mythical role as *psychopompe* [funereal animal].)

The dual nature of the symbol (it refers to both master and slave, white and black) is evident in *Cahier d'un retour au pays natal*, where Césaire, calling the white men "white dogs of the North," reminds them that the journey is not yet over: "Ecoutez, chien blanc du nord, serpent noir du / midi qui achevez le ceinturon du ciel / Il y a encore une mer à traverser" (*Cahier*, 151). And yet as a picture of the docile black, or, as whites call such a man, *"le très bon nègre,"* Césaire represents to us a black man crouched in a doghouse, barking for six long months like a French poodle. More precisely, the speaker in the poem remembers "la niche de Monsieur VAULTIER MAYENCOURT, où j'aboyai six mois de caniche" (*Cahier*, 131). Toward the end of the *Cahier* Césaire uses an expression that can refer to a servile dog when he says that it is not true that it is sufficient "that we heel – or keep pace – with the world" (*Cahier*, 139). But the *cynocephale* (dog-faced bat) appears in the *Cahier* as well. It may be that we are dealing here with the dog-faced monstrous man of legend, Saint Christopher in his earliest state, but the word more probably refers to the bat. Multiple readings are possible.

The symbolism of the dogs is, then, dual and troubling. We saw it used by Claude McKay. We should also note its use by Toni Morrison, in *Song of Solomon*, when Milkman visits Circe in the ruins of the white man's abode, surrounded by their dogs – sole vestiges of the white race's power and reign. In fact, we learn in an earlier passage that whites prize their dogs more than they do their blacks: "Dog races. White people did love their dogs. Kill a nigger and comb their hair at the same time. But I've seen grown white men cry about their dogs."[7] Of some bearing here, too, is the fact that in Lusophone African literature we have a collection of stories by Luís Bernardo Honwana entitled *Nós matamos o cão tinhoso* (*We Killed Mangy Dog*), in which the outcast dog, forming a relationship with a black boy who is suffering from alienation by other members of the society – whites, mulattoes, East Indians – becomes a key metaphor, but one that moves directly opposite from Morrison.[8]

* * *

A performance of Césaire's play has been broadcast on French radio by Sylvia Monfort et al., but evidently not successfully so (see Kesteloot and Kotchy 1973, 155). While *Christophe* has played in Montreal and Venice, *Une saison au Congo* in Toulouse, and *Une tempête* in Ivory Coast, one must suppose that even with the finest of actors, schooled in the rhythms of Caribbean speech and Caribbean cane dances, the somewhat arcane character of *Et les chiens se taisaient*, with its codified language issuing from the downswing of Césaire's surrealism, would be lost on the spectators. Although the meanings grow clearer at mid-play, time is nevertheless required – certainly more than the normal amount available to a playgoer – to analyze the significance of the omnipotent and omnipresent sun imagery – its rising and setting, central to Le Rebelle's energy, to life, to fertility. Likewise, one must meditate on the various implications of the "dogs," of the allegorical speakers. Time is required to understand the allusions to time, whose function in Césaire's theater, at least in its historic manifestations, has been meticulously and methodically analyzed by both Albert Owusu-Sarpong[9] and Kotchy (Kesteloot and Kotchy 1973, 145-56).

Such time is not available in a theater presentation, not even to the Martiniquais, who have the advantage of intimately knowing the flora and fauna Césaire alludes to. Therefore, the *dramatic* impact of this work would be attenuated in a live performance, while our reading of it brings along great pain and intensity of feeling. It is probable that in a live performance, therefore, we might well yearn for more action, but we would even so sense this tragic poem's lyric beauty and its general intentions and tone. Despite Kotchy's impression to the contrary (Kesteloot and Kotchy 1973, 153), most of us know what datura and flame trees are; most of us understand that a firefly can give off sparks like pieces of flint engaging. But we still do not grasp many an image and many a passage, precisely because the piece *is* lyric, drawn from deep in Césaire's psyche, beneath and beyond discourse. In this work Césaire is "le pêcheur roux des choses profondes et noires" (*AM*, 117; "the ruddy fisherman of deep black things"). We sense the pain and frustration far more than we are able to define cognitively the conjoined words. We must read, reread, consider, and reconsider this work in a way not available to us when we attend a play.

Et les chiens se taisaient is not a play, a conclusion with which Rodney Harris concurs, finding it to be a prolonging of Césaire's poetry.[10] We might call it the beginning of his dramatic phase, but we must wait for *La Tragédie du roi Christophe, Une saison au Congo,* and *Une tempête* for truly "attendable" plays. And even at that, *Christophe* is something of a transition between *Et les chiens se taisaient* and *Une saison au Congo,* just as *Et les chiens se taisaient* is something of a transition from poetry to drama and makes as fitting a conclusion to *Les Armes miraculeuses* as it does an introduction to Césaire's theater.

Et les chiens se taisaient is less presentable, less accessible than any play by Brecht, to whom Césaire is frequently compared, mainly because of the authors' similar use of history to show the errors of men's ways in living their everyday lives. In the form of an epic poem devoted to a conflict between the will to dominate and the will to be a hero, *Et les chiens se taisaient* stands next to the *Cahier* as a major work of twentieth-century French poetry, one of extreme profundity and stellar beauty. The breath of the *Cahier* moves through it, as evi-

denced in such lines as the following, delivered by Le Rebelle as he
becomes more forthcoming to his mother and describes his mission:

> je suis prêt
> sonore à tous les bruits et plein de
> confluences
> j'ai tendu ma peau noire comme une peau
> de bourrique. . .
> le tam-tam halète. le tam-tam éructe.
> le tam-tam crache
> des sauterelles de feu et de sang. Ma main
> aussi est
> pleine de sang. . .
> Je ne suis pas un coeur aride.
> Je ne suis pas
> un coeur sans pitié.
> Je suis un homme de soif bonne qui circule
> fou autour de mares
> empoisonées
>
> (I am ready
> sonorous to all the noises, and full of confluences
> I have stretched my black skin taut like the skin
> of a she-ass. . .
> the tom-tom gasps
> the tom-tom belches
> the tom-tom spits [out] grasshopper-sparks of fire and blood.
> My hand also is
> full of blood. . .
> I am not an arid heart. I am not a heart without pity.
> I am a man of honest thirst who circulates, mad, around
> poisoned ponds.)
>
> (AM, 102-3; my translation)

Many critics discuss the function of history in *Et les chiens se
taisaient,* but if history is at issue, it is history in the abstract, the
philosophy of history, that is under examination. With *Christophe*
and *Une saison au Congo* Césaire will present his material in a new
light, as a negritude historiographer. In these two plays he writes historical events into a wholly dramatic cadre. Of course his presentation of Toussaint in the *Cahier* revealed his interest in using historical figures as archetype, symbol, and exemplum.[11] By the time of the
composition of *Christophe* and of *Une saison* this interest has fully

matured and has also become a dramatic imperative. But it is safe to say that Christophe and Lumumba represent more than exempla. In fact, one might conclude that even though all the historical figures Césaire has chosen to portray fictionally fulfill his intention to divert and teach, and even though they often represent martyrdom and black authenticity, they also appear to have been chosen in light of their postrevolutionary, postcolonial positions and functions, thus demonstrating the historicity of the black race.

Although he lacks specificity, even Le Rebelle is fixed in "time after which"; his story concerns the aftermath of his first revolt, the murder of the master. The same can be said of the stories of Toussaint, Christophe, and Lumumba. History for Césaire is not only a tool of culture, a basis of nationalism or Africanism and a source of national consciousness, as Owusu-Sarpong asserts (23-24), but, more importantly, it is a vehicle through which he may examine the criminal record of the white man, demand an accounting, and express the urgent need for revolutionary action and redress.

Toussaint seems to have most dominated Césaire's muse whenever it fixes on history, but Césaire has not always drawn on black exempla. Violently opposed to the Vichy government, to any kind of dictatorship and oppression, including the vicious censorship to which their journal *Tropiques* was subjected, Césaire and his collaborators clearly saw the Hugo of *Les Châtiments* as a type of the revolutionary ideal. They viewed Rimbaud and Lautréamont as *sectaires*, models of passionate and legitimate bias bent on renunciation of the poetic and political status quo. Even so, Toussaint and Lumumba are the authentic, the brightly burning stars, the ascending doves that one should reach out to grasp and emulate. They are the unqualified heroes of Césaire's world; other figures are but coincidentally mentioned.

Le Rebelle, not historically documented, is the black hero in the abstract, in violent revolt against the colonial régime. Through him we learn that the humiliated colonized man frees himself in and through violence.[12] Because he is an abstraction, Le Rebelle also shows us that revolt is a collective vindication. Césaire's treatment of current events and history is unmistakable and time-honored, for his almost methodical use of history to locate positive and negative exempla was recommended by Montaigne, among others, and Montaigne in fact followed his own recommendations with considerable enthusiasm and frequency. In Montaigne Césaire has an illustrious predecessor and yet another kind of model, conscious or unconscious. Like the essayist, the poet often becomes fused with his subjects' identities, and like the essayist he also understands but rejects the negative examples he uncovers in the past.

Chapter Four

La Tragédie du roi Christophe

If in *La Tragédie du roi Christophe* Césaire turns to the question of postcolonial corruption, we are nonetheless impressed by the somewhat sympathetic portrait of a well-meaning but flawed black tyrant, and by the continued depiction of trapped, eternally exploited islanders. Slave ships are still focal in the dialogues; the image of the *pirogue* returns, as does that of the *lambi*.[1] Mother Africa is ascendant in the troubled psyche of the pretentious parvenu Henri Christophe, whose tragicomic depiction at times recalls the *grandes comédies* of Molière but here culminates in a tragic fall into madness, apoplexy, and suicide. This play, however, has its roots in Haitian history and must be considered in that context. As Henock Trouillet contends in his careful and methodical study, Christophe can only be understood in the context of the decolonization of Haiti and in conjunction with Jean-Jacques Dessalines and Toussaint Louverture.[2]

Act 1

The play opens with an in-progress fight between two cocks, "Pétion" and "Christophe,"[3] and the commentator proceeds to give a history of the men for whom these fowl have been named. Early in the nineteenth century and subsequent to the revolution mounted by Toussaint Louverture, two states existed in Haiti. Alexandre Pétion styled himself as president of the Republic of Haiti and set up headquarters in Port-au-Prince in the South. After the death of President Dessalines,[4] Christophe, refusing to become president and consequently the toy of the Haitian mulattoes, named himself King Henri I and ruled from Cap-Haitien in the North. According to the commentator (who delivers the prologue), the ex-slave and cook

Christophe, driven by ambition, had chosen to emulate white kings, particularly those of France, and especially Louis XIV and Louis XVI.[5] This parodic behavior will be an aspect of Christophe's undoing.

In scene 1 Christophe refuses to accept the title of president; his powers have been curtailed by the Senate, following the tyranny of Dessalines. To Christophe, this curtailment indicates distrust. He recognizes that the mulattoes of the Senate are maneuvering to install the mulatto Pétion as president. Scene 2 takes place in Cap-Haitien, in a public square near the harbor. A ship approaches. Hugonin, Christophe's jester and agent, mingles with the citizens. A market woman hawks her wares: *rapadou* (sugarcane), tafia, rum, tobacco, *tosso* (jerkey). Hugonin flirts with her. Vastey enters and converses with the others, claiming the French hold both blacks and republics in low esteem, that they scorn both Pétion and Christophe. Ironically, Haiti has two republics, so to gain the respect of the French it will have to show them a kingdom and a king. Christophe enters. He chides those present for being lazy and slovenly, promising that under him there will be reforms.

Scene 3 occurs in the palace. Vastey, Magny (the "Duke of Pleasance" and the king's master of ceremonies), and courtiers are present. The scene rests on a Molieresque parody of court manners (cf. scene 1). Discussion revolves around the likelihood that the French find Christophe and his court ridiculous. Yet, Vastey contends, civilization is defined by form, as their king Christophe well understands. On and after Christophe's entrance ceremoniousness is pushed to the point of absurdity, presided over by the master of ceremonies, who reiterates that they should heed their *démarche* (carriage). Suddenly Christophe addresses some painful realities: Haitians no longer know their real African names, their past, but this will not prevent them from reshaping their future along the lines of emancipation and a restructuring of society. From this scene we recognize that in this play satire and farce vie with tragedy. One is reminded of Léon-Gontran Damas's famous poem in which he expresses his sense of being ridiculous when all dressed up in his tuxedo, aping the white man. Still, the substructures of Christophe's character reveal the pathos of the man.

Scene 4 shifts to the cathedral, for the king's coronation, Archbishop Corneille Brelle presiding. Christophe, in a parody of his contemporary Napoleon, snatches the crown from the archbishop's hand and crowns himself. In what will turn out to be an empty vow, he swears to prevent Haiti from reverting to slavery and from any infringement on freedom. Ironically, he himself induces slavery and infringements on human rights.[6]

Scene 5 takes place on the battlefield where Magny confronts the rebel leader Metellus and asks him why he conspires against Christophe. Here is our link with Toussaint, a constant in the works of Césaire, a symbol of martyred negritude, a culture hero. Metellus claims to have been fighting in the camp of Toussaint, where, on the wild mountain trails they had seen "Hope," a woman who dances madly to stir their spirits. Metellus – schooled by Toussaint and committed to the principle that Haiti should be open to all the isles, to all the world's blacks, not an island to be claimed ("staked out"), exploited, and ruled by tyrants – rejects both Christophe and Pétion, the one a "brute," the other a "haughty skeptic." Metellus is therefore now willing to abandon his dream and to die at Magny's command. He is killed by Magny's officer.

Christophe arrives. He laments the bloodshed, loss, and disarray of the land; he is sickened by the odor. But in any case, he feels the end is in sight. In a passage originally making up scene 6, a soldier enters, carrying Pétion's two-cornered hat on his rifle. The others rejoice. Christophe expresses the wish to end the conflict with Pétion and to unite the people against a "more threatening danger" than Magny and the other officers can imagine. Magny expresses some skepticism: "I only hope your eyes aren't opened too late" (33).

Scene 6 takes place in the senate in Port-au-Prince. The opposition leader calls Christophe's monarchy a "caricature" – a charge we do not wonder at. He submits that the Republic and the Parliament may be equally so, in view of Pétion's secretiveness. (We sense Césaire's democratic philosophy underlying the opposition leader's words: a republic cannot be expected to survive covert activities.) The opposition leader asks Pétion what is being plotted now behind the nation's back. Pétion finally reveals that Christophe is planning the reunification of the island – under his crown, of course. Thus they would all become Christophe's subjects. Obviously, the deputies are hostile to such a proposition. Scene 7 finds Christophe on the battlefield. He compares Africa to Haiti, where blacks are now

pitted against blacks. He then tells Magny to give the troops the order to march to the North, to the Cape.

Scene 8 (originally scene 7) moves to Christophe's villa for an in-
progress banquet, which has been prepared to celebrate the first
anniversary of Christophe's coronation. Thus, a year has passed by
with this stagnating situation of a double government and opposing
leaders. Christophe discusses with his master of ceremonies the
pomp and circumstance of the coronation banquet held by the king
of France and attended by the queen and the entire court.
Christophe, not unlike M. Jourdain in Molière's *Le Bourgeois Gentil-
homme*, recognizes that he not only does not have a queen, but,
moreover, the banquet needs must lack the pomp of the French
king's. (Césaire has denied Christophe's likeness to Jourdain, comparing him instead, interestingly enough, to "General Idi Amin
Dada.")[7] If Christophe does not have a queen, and if his banquet will
lack a certain lavishness, he *does* have his court poet, Chanlatte, who
recites his ode to rum, calling it "the national beverage" (39). (The
play's original published draft contained dialogue between the
bishop and Christophe and between Chanlatte and Christophe and
an episode between Hugonin and Christophe, all of which have
been excised from the final edition.) Chanlatte, Jahn assures us, was
a real Haitian poet, who wrote for Christophe and whose verse is actually quoted by Césaire in this passage of the play.[8]

Subsequently (in a passage not present in the original version of
the play) a letter is brought from "Wilberforce" complimenting
Christophe and telling him to "sow the seeds of civilization" (40),
though that plant grows but slowly. Temporarily, the tone grows serious as Christophe cries out that they do not have time to wait when
the fate of the people is at stake, and so civilization must take seed
and grow rapidly.

Mme Christophe then urges Christophe not to ask too much of
the people and not to be too immoderate. She, a plain woman, a
"good black wife," fears her children will lose their father. Is she a
Philinte, a Mme Jourdain, to this play? If she is not a Philinte, she is
surely the voice of the future; her prophetic words prepare us for
Christophe's downfall.

Now very excited and serious, Christophe rehearses with lyric ef-
fusion the many abuses that have been heaped on blacks and declares that they must climb out of their pit. For this, they must have

leaders. He must, therefore, ask more of blacks than of other people, and more than other people might ask. Mme Christophe tells her husband he is like the big fig tree stifling all the vegetation around it. She recognizes his megalomania; she is aware of the ego trip in his "mission." (Frederick Ivor Case explains that the fig tree is a special consecrated tree of the *Loa,* Ogoun Shango.)[9] "A cursed fig tree," replies Christophe, for he knows that the tom-tom is beating and that the people are dancing while the ocelot lies ready to spring, the "hunter of men" stalking the oblivious dancers. To protect them from themselves he must have something more than a "priest's litany" or a wife's precautions.

This reference to a "priest's litany" makes little sense in this version of the play because the dialogue between the bishop and Christophe that would explain the reference has been excised. In the original version, the bishop recites Scripture, referring to Bethel, house of the Lord (Genesis 28:16-22 and Psalms 127:1.) In the original passage the bishop seeks to prove he is no *"père-savane"* and can indeed speak to God in Latin, as Christophe asserts one should. The bishop's message also evokes indirectly the story of Esau who sold his birthright to his brother Jacob for bread and a bowl of soup. The omission of the passage thus eliminates a rich subtext.[10]

After Christophe's outburst, in which he disparages the contributions of his entourage, he drives all the courtiers from the hall and demands that Martial Besse, his chief engineer, be sent to him. In the course of their dialogue, Christophe divulges to Besse his plans to build a palladium of liberty, a kind of "ship" that will cancel out the slaver. The ship theme is important in island culture, even more so to those peoples who have known the horror of being shipped across the seas and sold into slavery. In *Cahier d'un retour au pays natal* the slave ship is subverted by the vehicle of legitimate negritude voyage, the *pirogue,* it having reached the level of a powerful and viable symbol that would haunt neo-African literature for at least a generation or two. Christophe's "ship" will be the famous, impenetrable Citadel of Haiti, "a battleship of stone," built at great expense to the people and never used. It might well be called "Christophe's Folly." As the curtain falls on act 1, an illumined vision of the Citadel is projected, a manifestation of Christophe's hallucination.

Act 2

In scene 1 two peasants express their dissatisfaction with the current
political situation. After all, they had fought the revolution to drive
the whites off the island and have it for themselves – certainly not to
continue institutionalized slavery, "even for blacks." There is no
freedom, not even religious freedom, for they are unable to have a
voodoo meeting. A drummer enters and reads Christophe's proclamation whereby farmers are expected to perform their agricultural
duties with the same rigor as the armed forces do theirs, on pain of
arrest and punishment.[11]

Scene 2 moves to Christophe's palace, "Sans Souci," where
Christophe tells the archbishop that the latter's request for repatriation to France is not to his royal liking, but he will continue to consider it. In the original version of the play, scene 2 begins with conversations between Christophe and Vastey, Prezeau, Hugonin, and
Magny, conversations found in scene 4 of the later version. In these
conversations we learn that the Comte de Mont-Roui is whipping
peasants; Christophe orders that he be publicly whipped and dis-
membered. We also see that Christophe intends to push through his
plans for the Citadel. Thus all must work; blacks cannot assume that
the revolution is over and that they can just sit back and behave like
whites. The bishop and Christophe's dialogue about the bishop's
repatriation comes after this, followed by further scolding of the
peasants, who have been summoned to be chided for fornicating
while unmarried, jeopardizing the island's need for family stability.
Hugonin matches the peasants one to the other, on the spot.

Although in the original version of scene 3 Vastey and Franco de
Medina converse with Christophe about "la question de Saint-
Domingue" and Christophe's refusal to surrender to the French
(also about his plans for the death of Franco de Medina), in the later
edition scene 3 takes place in a drawing room at Cape Henry, in
which two upper-class ladies share with Vastey their perception that
tyranny now reigns throughout Haiti. The older lady asks the
younger to sing the ballad about Ourika, the heroine of a novel that
all Paris is reading and weeping over (53). Vastey feels that
Christophe is working to see to it that no black girl is ever treated
like Ourika. This scene, including the allusion to a novel that may

well be Sembène Ousmane's *La Noire de . . .* , makes up scene 5 of
the original version.[12]

At the beginning of the fourth scene we learn of the planning of
the Comte de Mont-Roui's punishment for mistreating the peasants,
also of Richard's punishment for dancing and Magny's for undigni-
fied ascent of the palace staircase four steps at a time. These pun-
ishments, like those ordered in Albert Camus's *The Stranger,* do not
fit the "crime" – if either dancing or dashing up stairs is a crime – and
of course are linked to tyrannical regimes, as Césaire clearly intends
to show. Hugonin's matching off of the peasants in the interest of a
more solid Haitian family life takes place here, in this later version.
Christophe then meets with the state council chairman, who is the
peasants' spokesman. The people are tired, says the chairman, which
infuriates Christophe, who decrees that everyone must work. Subsequently, the undoing of Franco de Medina, the French king's envoy,
is plotted. At the end of the scene Christophe points out that the
archbishop's appointment has never been confirmed by the pope.
This may justify Christophe's having him done away with,
"peacefully, in his bed, and with no bloodshed" (64).

Scene 5 takes place near the archbishop's palace. The archbishop is heard crying offstage. Passersby and a beggar comment. A
woman sings a litany to the Virgin. Then we are rapidly transported
in scene 6 to the site of the Citadel. Forced laborers – "free slaves" of
the kind that have come into the work forces of colonial regimes in
such places as Mozambique and Angola – complain as they work at
the building. A foreman prods them. Thus we see that little has
changed in this new society: the economy of servitude is still in
place, only the factory has replaced the plantation. This is another
theme common to negritude literature: the same abuse continues,
heaped not only on blacks but the whole laboring class.

Christophe enters. He begins working to show the others how
"an honest black man works" (68). He prods them with his words
and his example. Then lightning strikes the powder stores and lays
ruin to the Treasury building and the garrison. Still Christophe is un-
shaken.

Some material found in the later version's scene 1 was located in
scene 4 of the original. Moreover, the original act 2 had a seventh
scene, still the Citadel, which included dialogue about the assassination of Brell. (This discussion occurs in scene 4 of the later edition.)

In scene 8 of the original the "presenter" speaks of the Arbonite River, Haiti's central artery, as Christophe had in scene 4. The presenter's lyric speech evokes the river scene with its *rédayeurs* (raftsmen) and the sound of the *lambi*. The passage on the Arbonite, seemingly lost from the final version, is reminiscent of the poetic majesty of *Cahier d'un retour au pays natal* and calls to mind the magnificent Langston Hughes poem "The Negro Speaks of Rivers."[13] But the passage also forms an intertext with Césaire's own poem of the river, "Your portrait," in *Corps perdu.*

Act 3

Scene 1 takes us to the royal palace. Courtiers and ladies are dancing. An old man vaunts the present state of Haitian society while Hugonin responds with sarcasm. Trou-Bonbon, Magny, and Vastey enter. We learn that with the Citadel still incomplete, Christophe is demanding that the people construct a new castle near Crête-à-Pierrot. Christophe and his "queen" enter with great fanfare. In his retinue are five African males dressed in *boubous* of red, yellow, and green, Christophe's favorite colors. The king tells how he bought the Africans free from a slaveship. He calls them "bonbons royaux" (royal gumdrops). Dialogue that can only be labeled *précieux* ensues between Christophe and some ladies, whom he also considers "bonbons royaux," the "délices" of his reign. Further play on language occurs when Guerrier enters with his wife. Magny now informs the king that Pétion proposes to sell plots of land. Here the new archbishop, Juan de Dios (Gonzales), enters and expresses to the king his hope that he and all the people of the Cape will join in the Feast of the Assumption, a holy day of obligation in the Catholic church and a great feast day. Christophe informs the clergyman that he will be in Limonade (lemonade) if the archbishop wishes to celebrate there.

Scene 2 is devoted to the celebration of the Feast of the Assumption in the Church of Limonade, with the five Congolese and the entire court in attendance. The litany of the Virgin and elements of the Mass are chanted in alternating choruses and mixed with voodoo prayers by Christophe. At the end of this scene, just as Archbishop Juan de Dios prays for the physical and spiritual health of the con-

gregation, we witness the emotional crisis of the king, who cries out
to "St. Toussaint" and "St. Dessalines," thus incorporating them into
the canon and folding their respective passions (in the sense of sufferings) into his feverish prayers. After seeing the ghost of the assassinated Brell – in a guilt-ridden vision reminiscent of Mac-
beth's – Christophe collapses, asking, "Who has put Bakula Baka on
me?" (79). (Bakula Baka is an insatiable voodoo demon who takes
vengeance on those who break their pacts, which tie them to a *Loa.*)
Not only has Christophe not carried out his oath to fight off slavery,
but he has even reinstated it with his tyrannical, autocratic use of
forced labor to accomplish his vainglorious goals.

Scene 3 takes place in the sacristy. Surrounded by his retinue,
Christophe is being tended by Dr. Steward, who predicts to Mme
Christophe that Christophe will survive but will be permanently par-
alyzed. After much thundering, Christophe proclaims himself intact
and firm, the "living image of our Citadel" (81) and determined to
carry on his projects. He is still demanding work and more work,
obedience, subservience. And he now defies the gods, brandishing
in their faces his *récade,* a type of scepter carried by African kings. It
too has become symbolic, standing for African tradition and African-
style authority. Christophe's *récade* seems to send out conflicting
messages: its regal meaning has been blemished by Christophe's
reign of terror.

In scene 4 Christophe is on his throne, old and feeble. From his
courtiers and Hugonin Christophe learns that Boyer (Mme Pétion's
lover and Pétion's successor) has advanced on his kingdom, that
Christophe's generals have deserted, and that Magny has been
bought off. Still Christophe does not give up. The original scene 4
contains a short dialogue between soldiers and peasants; the original
scene 5 contains some of the material now found in the present
scene 4. Christophe and Richard are here discussing the fatigue of
the soldiers and the sin of sedition that passes through the kingdom.
Christophe is also angry that people have been dancing at a ball
while he is sick. Their punishment will be to walk to church barefoot
for 15 successive days – quite a severe penance for their "sin." But
then Christophe is jury, judge, hangman, as well as priest and even
pope. (Note, however, that when Christophe says he has challenged
Saint-Pierre, Case contends he refers not to Saint Peter or the pope
but to the *Loa* spirit Saint-Pierre, who bears some of the Yoruba god

Shango's characteristics. But remember that Christophe has also challenged Saint Peter of Rome [the pope] in the person of the bishop.)

In scene 5 Hugonin describes the present anarchy of the people and the ruination of the land. Says Christophe, "Every one of your words is weighted down with the wreckage of my dreams" (87). Christophe explains what he has tried to do and recognizes it is time for the old king to lie down. Christophe's images now are drawn from his African past. Words such as *baobab, Congo, datura, toucan, raffia,* and *palm* flow through his speech like pegs on which he hangs his Afro-Caribbean identity. He calls on Africa to rouse his blood, his heart the "drum of [his] blood" (89).

Christophe then dresses and calls for his horse to be saddled as he prepares to meet the enemy once more. But he falls. In the throes of hallucinations, he asks Africa to wash him clean and to help him "go home" (back to Africa). Here, as so often is the case in black literature, Africa is the lost paradise, to which, for example, the old Martiniquais-African in Joseph Zobel's *Rue Cases-Nègres* is presumed to have returned after death. Christophe then takes out a revolver.

In scene 6 Hugonin is alone on stage and slightly tipsy. He calls for a minute of silence from the audience. Offstage we hear a shot (scene 11 in the original version). The final scene (scene 7) takes place at the construction site of the Citadel. "The King is dead" is echoed. Peasants carry the king's body into the Citadel. Vastey, the queen, and the African page enter. Christophe is to be buried upright in the mortar of the fortress. We learn from the page that Christophe is now assimilated to Shango, a power that "rides through the halls of heaven, mounted on the flaming ram of the tempest" (95). Forever a "king erect," as Vastey puts it, Christophe is the phoenix, crowned with gold: his spirit is immortal. As the African would say, "oba ko so" ("the king is not dead; his spirit is immortal"). We might be tempted to view the standing corpse and the phoenix as themes of renaissance and return as suggested at the end of *Et les chiens se taisaient,* but these two features allude to the Yoruba voodoo cult of Shango and to Christophe's chosen crest, which features the gold-crowned "phénix de gueules" against a blue sky studded with gold stars (Case, 21-23). Thus the issue is one of sociohistorical documentation. The standing corpse must account for Christophe's actions toward the living – that is, his spirit cannot

join the ancestors in their "resting place" but must remain account-
able to the living, as Case contends (21), while the phoenix as
metaphor of rebirth is more the appropriation of Christophe than of
Césaire.

Analysis

There is no escaping the difficulties presented by this complex play,
first when it comes to establishing the text itself and then to arriving
at a "correct" or even "best" interpretation of it. There is, first of all,
the problem of variants. The link between the historical figure
Christophe and his modern counterparts embodied in the Duvalier
dictators is easy enough to make, and the Royal Dahomets of
Christophe are readily equated to the Tontons Macoute, the Duvaliers' vicious police force evoked in the poetry of René Depestre and
who have perhaps been somewhat weakened recently in meeting
with strong resistance from the Haitian people. The absoluteness of
these dictatorships, in which even the "Our Father" of the Lord's
Prayer (required to be recited in the country's schools) was modified
to "Our Doc," is not equalled by Christophe, yet the proclivities are
all too identifiable.[14] Similarly, Hegelian and Sartrean notions of the
master-slave syndrome are self-evident, but what can we say of the
portrait of Christophe, which combines in one person buffoon and
king, Lear and his Fool?

René Ménil considers Christophe a romantic, not an exploiter,
whereas Hervé Fuyet et al. see his romanticism as a coverup for his
fundamentally exploitative nature.[15] I would have to lean with the
Fuyets here. But their understanding of Christophe's labor policies
entail Marxist ideologies that seem incompatible with the thrust of
the play. Moreover, they have identified in this play the negritude
theme of community-in-suffering, here connected with the theme of
work as a regenerating force, and they find this dimension
"anachronistic." Joppa and Owusu-Sarpong see Christophe's sever-
ity not as gratuitous but as an accommodation to the draconian tac-
tics needed to raise the black from his peculiar situation, oppressed
by both white and mulatto.

Still, the play is to some extent a near satire of all dictatorship
and an indictment of abusive postcolonial black regimes. Although

more comic,[16] Christophe is, among other things, a rough draft of Mobutu, who emerges in the wake of Lumumba's death in *Une saison au Congo*. There is a kernel of German fascism in Christophe's fanatical work policies, for does he not enslave the black over and above the mulatto, already *affranchi?* His policies have an element of racism recognized by Fuyet et al. Christophe's idea is less that "work engenders man" (as Engels had it) and more that "*Arbeit macht Frei*" (as the Nazis had it). The words suit the concentration-camp atmosphere of the Citadel scenes. Besides, Césaire's former allegiance to Marxist-Leninist ideologies that Fuyet et al. invoke to support their commentary is not as crucial here as is the poet's hatred of fascism.

We have something of a psychodrama in *Christophe*. The evolution, or devolution, of Christophe, part-dreamer, part-fool, is dynamically portrayed. In the Dunn interview Césaire claims that the buffoon in Christophe is only superficial, that behind these somewhat ridiculous things there is grandeur. In the absurd ceremoniousness of Christophe's court, which parodies that of the kings of France, Césaire assuredly means to be satirizing display. As Chevrier says, Césaire intends to "denounce the sumptuous ostentation of certain presidential courts [even of today], and the grotesque etiquette ill-adapted to the climate, as to the very mode of African life" (Chevrier, 172). The purpose is not so much to produce the "rire nègre" or "rire africain" that we occasionally observe elsewhere in Césaire's work as to satirize outward display (*une satire du paraître*), an unfortunate if occasional outcome of independence.

For Césaire, however, Christophe is Promethean. He insists on Christophe's isolation and *échec* (fall) (Dunn, 3-4). Still, Christophe, *enragé* if not *engagé*, acts and reacts in terms of external pressures from opponents, populace, and clergy. As Maximilien Laroche says, "Christophe's politics are a balancing act on a tightrope stretched over a lions' den."[17]

Christophe's tragedy is more accurately understood in terms of his inner disposition, which embraces intransigence, autocracy, arrogance, isolationism, and ambition. Laroche assists our understanding of the play's title by explaining that the word *tragedy* should be interpreted in a Haitian context; it thus becomes the equivalent of *échec*. In fact, the idea does not seem far from the Greek concept of hamartia. Chevrier agrees with Laroche on this

matter of *échec:* abandoned by the blacks, not understood by the
people, and betrayed by his own corrupt entourage, Christophe falls
(Chevrier, 173). And, he adds, falls were predicted by Fanon as early
as 1960.

In any case, Christophe *must* fall: the dictates of good faith
would demand it were the outcome not determined by historical fact
alone. Because the play is a historical drama of sorts, it is very difficult to understand why some critics have allowed themselves to see
the face of Césaire behind the mask of Christophe. At best, the story
could represent the fears a great leader such as Césaire might have in
his brush with power.

It is interesting to note, though, how the pallbearers at the end
of *Christophe* complain that the body is not only heavy but is getting
heavier. Thus, Christophe is a historical burden for the Haitian people, who have the oldest democracy in our hemisphere but
nonetheless, and very ironically, have known unending repression at
home from a series of bloody dictatorships as well as pressure from
external powers, chiefly the United States. Their burden is their
historical load, not their cultural load.[18]

In *Christophe* we are dealing with the tragedy of a failed dream,
of flawed and misguided leadership – one of the more negative phenomena of revolutionary societies and one often studied in recent
African novels. As Césaire says, "It is easier to grab hold of one's independence than to build a world on new bases."[19] Grand-scale issues of justice are at stake in this play, for fundamentally the tragedy
is not only that of Christophe "rushing grandiosly and heroically to
death" but of the colonized, decolonized, and recolonized Haitian
people.

In his speech before the First International Congress of Black
Writers in Paris in 1956, Césaire denounced the call of the white
world for a renunciation by blacks of their African traditions and for
a turn to progress. He cited the example of Hawaiian prince
Kamehameha II's effort to subvert the Hawaiian culture and its traditional gods: "Among us," he said, "there will be no Kamehameha
II."[20] Clinging to African traditions in his politics, Christophe
nonetheless calls for a harsh work ethic. He fails not so much from
his policy (which may have some compromises inherent in it) as from
internal ambition. Christophe is the counterpart to Zaire President
Mobutu Sese Seko and the extreme opposite of *Une saison au*

Congo's Patrice Lumumba, who is destroyed by external forces. While Christophe fuses in his being the pure and the impure, Lumumbu is a pure, archetypal tragic figure, like Toussaint. Lumumba's story, real though it is (or perhaps because it *is* real), has all the earmarks of a Greek tragedy – that of Oedipus, for example, caught in the twin vises of destiny and the polis. The story of Lumumba was ripe for the telling from a negritude perspective when Césaire undertook his play in 1967. *Une saison au Congo* is a more profound, or at least more successful, play than *Christophe*, though it consequently lacks *Christophe*'s peculiar modernity. *Christophe*'s ambiguity makes it black comedy, a twentieth-century tragicomedy – a play of Brechtian stamp if ever there was one.

Chapter Five

Une saison au Congo

Césaire's plays increasingly draw the reader into the arena of action as his theater becomes less theoretical, abstract, and hermetic and more discursive and dramatic. Even though the reader becomes, in the words of Bernard Zadi-Zaourou, a "second narrator,"[1] and even though the plays' lines sharpen and become more ascendant, the rhythmic mechanisms never falter. And this African-Caribbean rhythm enlists as well the participation of the reader audience, just as Zadi-Zaourou has claimed. This rhythm is, of course, functional in Césaire's first two plays, but in his third, *Une saison au Congo* of 1965, rhythm, a clearly defined tragic focus of catalyst and catastrophe, and a clearly victimized and largely sympathetic hero all come together to form what some consider Césaire's most accomplished drama.

Une saison au Congo reminds us that when we deal with Césaire's plays, we are always dealing with a poet. Ronnie Scharfman puts it well when she contends that Césaire's plays might never have been written if the poetry had not preceded them. Yet Césaire's drama is often studied in preference to his poetry, partially because the situation from which the text emanates is dramatic rather than lyrical. While Jacques Chevrier sees a contradiction between the two forms of *engagement* assumed by Césaire – the *engagement* of the militant and that of the poet (181-84) – I believe the two are quite reconcilable, at least in Césaire's cosmos. In *Une saison au Congo* it is obvious that the hero, if not the other characters, has both.

The superiority of this play over the others is arguable, despite the fact that the historical theme of decolonization once more has dominion, this time manifested in an African-style colonialism. As in *Christophe* and *Une tempête*, Césaire seems to be asserting not only that revolution and decolonization are drastically needed but also that violence is inevitable, just as solidarity is necessary for revolution to be mounted. This is what Frantz Fanon prescribed in *Toward the African Revolution*: that only violence can wash away humiliation and, over and above that precept, Africa must be freed and unified.[2] Moreover, Fanon contends in *The Wretched of the Earth*, the black bourgeoisie may be one of the principal stumbling blocks to this decolonization.

Indeed, *Une saison au Congo* does showcase the historical failure of the Congolese to achieve that freedom and unity. The failure comes in the form of a crisis in postrevolutionary leadership, much as it does in *Christophe*. In *Une saison au Congo*, however, Patrice Lumumba's tragedy is more starkly depicted than is Henri Christophe's. The hero Lumumba is destroyed not by any flaws in his personality but by the ambitious Mokutu, a thinly disguised caricature of Mobutu Sese Seko, the current president of Zaire, in concert with the imperialist Belgian, French, and American forces.[3] Here we cannot easily fault the tragic hero, and so we cannot quite agree with Marcel Odden's contention that "Patrice Lumumba, in *A Season in the Congo*, finds himself in a situation that is quite close to that of Christophe."[4] Césaire senses a difference between the two protagonists, for he says in the interview with Donald Dunn that Lumumba, more than Christophe, is characterized by nobility and tragic grandeur: his is a rush to the grave, to *échec* (Dunn, 5). Lumumba knows he will fall but moves forward with that knowledge. Yet, for Césaire, Christophe also has grandeur, "in spite of his methods" (Dunn, 9), which Césaire cannot endorse.

Lumumba's martyrdom has a didactic and iconographic function. He is *engagé*, pure and Christ-like in an impure and wicked world, and by that he is like Le Rebelle of *Et les chiens se taisaient*. This faultlessness highlights Lumumba's tragedy, but we must also remember that the degree to which his martyrdom is a triumph over ontological givens makes him slightly less tragic – by some people's definitions – than a defeated Christophe, an ill-fated Oedipus, a tempestuous Phèdre. Césaire's objectives might be linked to Kierkegaard, who emphasized action and decision and maintained that we commit ourselves to a way of life, that we choose ourselves. Lumumba is probably more Corneillean than Racinean, although I do not suggest that Césaire's play is grounded in continental literature. On the contrary (and as Frederick Ivor Case would have it), we owe it to Césaire to have created an authentically "Negro" style, even while using French, the language of colonizer and missionary, in his negation of these very types.[5] As in the *Cahier* and as Sartre contends in "Orphée noir," Césaire molded the French language to his uses, syntactically, lexically, and rhythmically, and then turned it against those who had imposed their linguistic systems on him. If any valid comparison of *Une saison au Congo* with continental literature exists, it is, as Jonathan Ngaté has shown, with the pre-African Rimbaud, not only in regard to Césaire's title, evocative of Rimbaud's *Une saison en enfer,* but because the poets share sensibilities that are revolutionary in a philosophical, social, and aesthetic sense.[6] Rimbaud not only said "Je est un autre" but also, in "Mauvais Sang," "je suis un nègre" ("'I' is another," "I am a Negro").

Une saison au Congo, like the *Cahier* and Césaire's other plays, went through many revisions, according to Rodney Harris.[7] Built on contemporary history, this play has as its pivotal heroic victim a man of mythical, larger-than-life proportions. By its very title *Une saison au Congo* is no more about one person than it is about a whole people caught in a particular historical moment, "a season seasoned with blood," as Frédérique Dutoit has so aptly put it.[8] Césaire has insisted on this principle of "generality" (as quoted in Owusu-Sarpong, 139).

Une saison au Congo consists of three acts that flesh out three basic stages in Lumumba's political career: conquest, crisis, and assassination. Here one is reminded of Danton, Robespierre, and Stalin, more so than in *Christophe*, where anxiety is such a significant part of the tragic load. Examples of those "culture heroes" of whom I have spoken—Toussaint, Kenyatta, Senghor, Martin Luther King, and Nelson Mandela—are called to mind here. Fanon speaks of these culture heroes in *The Wretched of the Earth*, pointing out, as does Owusu-Sarpong (186), that the vindication the culture hero seeks is of a primordial exigency.[9] Moreover, this individual has certain attributes that qualify him for the task: he is an *homme de culture*—a hero *to* the culture and *for* the culture—and is revered by the people because he has played the historical role of affirming and vindicating the culture. More importantly, he has healing powers. Lumumba is, by his ordeal and passion, such a hero and even reminds us of Aristotle's virtuous man. He is temperate, courageous, and just—both for his own sake and for the sake of others.

Act 1

The Belgians' oppressive policies are unequivocally spelled out in the opening of the play, with Lumumba as the *bonimenteur* (beer salesman) urging people in the African quarter of Leopoldville to "drink, drink, drink,"[10] for the Belgians have taught the Congolese to drink beer but not to govern themselves. The people have not been allowed to experience any other freedom. The basic human right to congregate and attempts to emigrate or to record one's thoughts all bring prison. Polar Brand beer is, in fact, the only pleasure allowed, and so, Lumumba, pictured as the beer salesman he was as a young man, is selling the beer while putting a torch to the company. He is the go-between for the company (the rich, the elite) and the buyer (the masses, the poor). As he hawks his wares, onlookers retort, and Belgian policemen (the "cops") consider but refrain from questioning him. Ultimately, they consider "that Nigger" dangerous, since the government is involved, after all, in the capitalist venture of backing the Polar Beer that Lumumba is attempting to sell.

The sanza player, considered another nuisance by the police, begins to sing *"Ata-ndele"* ("Sooner or later" [3]). He will reappear throughout the play, providing a lyrical side to this political tragedy; he is a link character, similar to the Greek chorus. David Dunn views him as functioning to distance the protagonists from their public, which is a Brechtian technique.[11] Césaire has stated that the sanza player represents the people, or the good common sense of the people (Dunn, 9).

In scene 2 an African bar is being set up. Offstage a voice proclaims that the buffalo (the Belgian government) is wounded. At the bar prostitutes solicit, and all complain of the Belgians. Mokutu enters, dressed in European clothing and looking like a pimp. He announces that the Belgians have arrested Patrice. Meanwhile, he says, far off in Brussels the fate of the Congo is being decided. He endorses the revolt of the black African politicians. A woman at the bar, Mama Makosi, the "Mighty Madame," proposes that they work to raise bail for Patrice, so that he can "sit at the table in Brussels with the rest of them" (7).

In scene 3 the action shifts to the prison in Elisabethville, where Lumumba is held. One of the Belgian jailers quotes Lumumba's poetry to his face and punches him in the ribs. The jailers then ridicule him for an article he has written demanding his freedom and asking to sit at the round-table conference in Brussels. Both jailers strike Lumumba again and continue to ridicule him. The warden enters and tells Lumumba he is to be sent to Brussels as president of the National Congo Movement.

Scene 4 is set in Brussels, where a group of bankers is discussing how the Belgian government has, at Lumumba's request, set the date for Congolese independence at 30 June 1960, which for them is a portent of "ruin." They decide that they can prevent this by buying out the Congolese leaders. This plan to corrupt the African leaders will be one of the chief obstacles to the liberation of the Congo. An element of satire figures in this scene: the bankers, dressed in "monkey suits," are speaking in free verse; the devise gives their dialogue a parodic and farcical, if not ridiculous, cast.

Scene 5 returns us to Leopoldville, where the crowd is celebrating independence. Still, we discover in this scene the next great obstacle to freedom: tribal disputes. Says Mpolo (here called "A Man"), "From now on, we're all just plain Congolese" (15). He then proposes to drink to peace, either with Polar (Belgian) beer or Primus (African) beer.

In scene 6 (elsewhere in Leopoldville) Basilio, king of Belgium, and General Massens, commander of the Congolese militia, converse in front of the curtain. Basilio considers the black African a "savage" who, with independence, will revert to his pre-Christian barbarism, and thus all the work of the Belgian missionaries will be undone. Massens proposes that Basilio convey to the people the idea that their freedom is a gift from him and not a right that they have conquered, or reconquered.

The curtain rises revealing Lumumba, Kala Lubu, other delegates and a crowd of Congolese. At Kala Lubu's suggestion the crowd hails Basilio, calling him Bwana Kitoko, king of Belgium, but they also hail King Kala, president of the newly formed Congolese Republic. Basilio pompously speaks of his predecessors, especially King Leopold, who came to the Congo, he says, to bring civilization. (Also to gain control of the copper mines and the Congo's other mineral wealth.) Basilio very paternalistically assures the crowd that the Congolese can count on the Belgians' "disinterested assistance" (18).

Kala Lubu warns the crowd that independence does not validate lawlessness; independence has come, he says, "under the twofold

guidance of custom and civilization . . . to reconcile the old and the
new, the nation and its tribes" (19). In a somewhat celebrated
speech (anthologized and translated in Collins's *Black Poets in
French* [223-37]), Lumumba evokes the sufferings of black Africans
under Belgian rule. He reminds the crowd of their servitude and cel-
ebrates their victory over it. He poetically sings the praises of Africa,
whose heart is "Congo," whose mother is "Congo," whose child is
"Congo." Congo also suggests the word *Kongo* – "power," the chief
and the hunter whose totem is panther. Lumumba concludes his
speech by promising rebirth for Kongo – a new age in which laws will
be remade and customs revised – and calling for political and spiritual union: "For Kongo! Uhuru! Freedom!" (19-20).

The four bankers, Lumumba, the sanza player, and Mokutu converse in the next panel of this scene. The bankers are shocked by
Lumumba's speech and decry its virulence. Mokutu sides with them
on this issue but claims that he intends to fight against colonialism
with Lumumba. The fifth banker enters and advises the other
bankers to adopt the new ideology of "self-determination." But his
advice is charged with irony, for he is actually speaking of the Belgians as "determining" what will become of the mineral wealth of
the province of Katanga (its uranium, copper, diamonds, cobalt).

Scene 7 takes place in a nightclub. From a radio a woman's voice
can be heard calling for Africans to "get to work," for the
"mobilization of the working classes must be total, unconditional,
deliberate, voluntary" (25). Then another voice is heard, also urging
the people of the Congo to wake up and fight for their independence. Congolese soldiers, some half-drunk, invade the stage shouting, "Down with politicians! Down with Lumumba" (25).

Scene 8 takes place in the prime minister's office in Leopoldville,
where Lumumba is calling for help. He claims that all must become
slaves for Congo, working 24 hours a day. Mpolo warns Lumumba
that the soldiers (black Congolese whom Lumumba regards as
"Belgians" because they behave like Belgians) are approaching and
shouting for his death. Lumumba's black brothers appear to be overcome by their own personal ambition, and Mokutu has become their
choice for secretary of state. Not yet does Lumumba understand,
however, that Mokutu is one of his chief enemies, for he says, "You
want Mokutu? Good. I ratify your choice. . . . Mokutu's my friend, my
brother. I know that Mokutu will never betray me. . . . Well, I appoint

Mokutu" (30). Lumumba then tells the soldiers to be prepared to do battle with the "enemy, the hawk" (i.e., the Belgians).

In scene 9 white refugees are being driven from the Congo. Voices are sending messages over the radio. Basilio and Massens appear. Massens wants order restored, even if by force (and therefore in opposition to international law). This order must prevail, for otherwise European lives (*human* lives) are at stake. Basilio agrees, and Massens gives the command to the Belgian paratroopers to attack. Tom-toms spread the news of the attack.

In scene 10 Lumumba, Kala, and a pilot are flying over Elisabethville in a plane; it is storming. The Katanga authorities are not allowing them to land. Lumumba, claiming *he* is the authority, orders the pilot to land; the pilot refuses. Ultimately Kala tells the pilot to head for Leopoldville, while Lumumba tells him to head for Moscow, where he hopes to get arms. (The conflict between Kala and Lumumba, which will be fatal, is already apparent here. Moreover, the despicable and mercenary role of the two superpowers in African affairs and notably in the struggle for control of the Congo, especially Katanga, begins to unfold).

Senators at the Congolese parliament discuss in scene 11 the deterioration of the Congo and its coffers. They complain that their leaders are never there, always flying about. Lumumba protests, saying that they do not travel enough. He maintains that the Belgian ambassador, Mynher Van den Putt, is doing everything in his power to undermine the new republic, while General Massens has been preparing for raids. The treaty with the Belgians, then, means nothing. Moreover, there is a new development: Tzumbi and Msiri, financed and counseled by the Belgians, have declared Katanga an independent state allied with Belgium. Lumumba's dream of African unity is in danger. An appeal to the United Nations has brought forth the promise that Secretary General Dag Hammarskjöld will arrive tomorrow. Again he appeals to his black "brothers" to fight the "monster" (37).

By scenes 12 and 13 Hammarskjöld, quite pompous and, more seriously, somewhat impractical, has arrived. Poet that he is, he quotes a passage from Saint-John Perse's "Winds." (Perse was, of course, Césaire's compatriot, and some aspects of their poetry are not unalike.) In an ensuing speech Lumumba claims to be neutral and to have come in order to solve the problems of the Congo by conciliation and diplomacy. The Ambassador of the Grand Occident decries rocking-chair politics and declares that if the United Nations is there to police the world, it is also there to put out fires, including the flames of communism, wherever they flare up.

Act 2

Scene 1 reverts to the African bar, with the prostitutes and Mama Makosi moving about, while Lumumba, Mokutu, and their friends converse. Lumumba recalls the arrival of the Europeans to the Congo and asserts that it was exactly then that the Congo began to disintegrate: state, family, and people. This passage in particular indicts the Europeans for the waste they laid to African culture and the conflicts they created in this culture by forcing their values and religion. Christianity once again is called into question. Lumumba declares, as did Nietzsche and Dostoyevski, that "God is dead" (45).

In scene 2 we have a meeting of the Congolese cabinet, attended by Lumumba, Mpolo, Mokutu, and Croulard, Lumumba's Belgian secretary. Isaac Kalonji appears before the cabinet to urge the seizure of Bakwanga, site of the diamond mines. Mokutu seconds the suggestion, pointing out that funds are dried up and that his soldiers have not been paid in two months. Mokutu confesses that a rivalry has arisen between himself and Mpolo, who aspires to replace him as colonel. Lumumba states emphatically that it is Mokutu who will be chief of staff.

The chief of police enters and informs Lumumba that Bishop Gabriel Makoso has just published in *Christian Conscience* an article in which he has denounced Lumumba as an atheist. Mpolo reads the article aloud. Lumumba, now ready for war with any enemy, tells the police chief to arrest Makoso and shut down his paper. Indeed, he goes as far as to order that the army arrest anyone, white or black, who causes unrest. For the time being, the main problem is Katanga. Lumumba plans to confer with Hammarskjöld; meanwhile, he says, Tzumbi, leader in Katanga and a "traitor" (and modeled after Moise Tschombe), had "better say his prayers" (50).

In scene 3 Lumumba, in his office, complains to Hammarskjöld that the United Nations has not expelled the Belgians from the Congo and that it is holding diplomatic conversations with the traitor

Tzumbi. Hammarskjöld, however, feels no obligation to Lumumba. The loss of Katanga by secession would be a great misfortune for the Congo, says Lumumba, and therefore the Congolese Republic will attempt to prevent it by force. He requests planes from the United Nations for this mission, and Hammarskjöld flatly refuses. Then, says Lumumba, the Congolese will be obliged to request Soviet assistance.

Scene 4 intimates civil war, here allegorized and speaking of African spiritism. The Congolese prepare for battle. The scene provides transition between Lumumba's efforts to negotiate with the inhabitants of Katanga through the United Nations and his war with the secessionists, for in scene 5 we learn that Lumumba's troops, after persecuting and killing thousands of Balubas, have taken Bakwanga, and that Kalonji has fled. For this violence, Kala reports, world opinion is against the Congolese, and the United Nations is outraged. Lumumba, however, asks where the United Nations was when the Belgians were killing the Congolese and pitting the tribes against each other.

Scene 6 – one of the play's most moving – is danced by Lumumba and Hélène Bijou as they speak highly poetic lines about how dance is a fundamental form of human expression, bound to the life force and involving fertility and vitality. It is the dance of the peacock, a *pavane*. This scene provides the play with its title, for Lumumba says,

> We have danced the dance of my life! When I am gone, when I am
> spent like the blinding blind meteor in the night sky,
> when the Congo is no more than a season seasoned with blood,
> be beautiful, still beautiful, keeping
> of the terrible days no more
> than the few drops of dew that make
> the hummingbird's plumes more beautiful
> for having traversed the storm. (60)

Out of chaos and suffering comes greater beauty and meaning.

This lyrical sequence is dropped in scene 7, in which we find Kala delivering a monologue in the president's palace. Kala feels he must pull in the reins on Lumumba; he would like to think that he controls him. He fears that some regard Lumumba as a communist, and he knows that in protecting him he is viewed as aiding and abetting the Communist International. Still, he knows that Lumumba is

not a communist and that he has even avoided contacting
Khrushchev to avoid the label. Kala decides that he will seek the help
of Bishop Malula and Mokutu in controlling Lumumba. And it is not
at all by accident that the sanza player at the end of this scene sings
of the chameleon and his darting tongue.

In scene 8 we find Lumumba speaking his innermost thoughts to
his wife, Pauline, who well knows her husband has been betrayed by
his so-called friends, who she says are only waiting for the chance to
knife him or to sell him for a "mess of pottage." She finds Mokutu
untrustworthy, for, after all, as she reminds her husband, Mokutu
was an informer for the Belgians. In light of this aggressive role, we
cannot at all accept Clément Mbom's interpretation of the part
Césaire envisions for women in the salvation of the race.[12] Mbom
argues largely from the African perspective of woman "who does not
exist outside of the man, etc."(237), although he does, if only barely,
recognize that Césaire may well be perceiving the modern black
woman as a political agent. But Mbom does not reckon with the
African type represented by such real female figures as Winnie
Mandela or Bessie Head.

If Lumumba wants to see only the good in Mokutu we must assume that this owes not to Lumumba's innocence but to his gen-
erosity. Here the hero reminds us of the Corneillean rather than the
Racinean tragic victim. But Lumumba's sense of security based on
the fact that Kala will protect him as long as they stick together is
truly unfounded and, of course, ironic, for we have just seen that
Kala is out to get Lumumba. Again Pauline is on the mark when she
points out to her husband that Kala is probably jealous of him.

Lumumba wishes to change the scene; he picks up his guitar and
begins to sing a Swahili song ("Don't depend on the rotting tree"
[67]). He falls asleep and has a nightmare in which a bishop, Kala
and Mokutu appear (stage front), with Kala and Mokutu as kneeling
apparitions. From the bishop's call for a Christian reaction to perse-
cution we know that he seeks liberty in a religion that has used every
means of denying it. As Case has pointed out, the most dangerous
man of all may well be the black intellectual who has been domesti-
cated and christianized with greatest efficacy. At any rate, the bishop
here is a dangerous man: he has not only sold himself but is a subject for pity because he is an unconscious victim, given over to an
adoration of the white world and its religion. Pauline now tries to

awaken Lumumba. She turns on the radio to hear Kala Lubu announce that Lumumba has betrayed his trust and that he, Kala, is therefore appointing Joseph Iléo prime minister and empowering him to form a new government. Lumumba has fallen victim to a coup d'état.

In scene 9 Lumumba swears to get rid of King Kala; Mpolo agrees that it is time to strike. Lumumba has lost interest in the ineffectual United Nations; he will call on the Ghanaians for aid. And indeed in scene 10, which takes place in the Radio Building, we learn that the military from Ghana has been sent to the Congo to restore order. As a result, the Ghanaian colonel informs Lumumba that he is not to broadcast his speech on the radio, since no political faction is to be given access to the radio, under the strict orders of Matthew Cordelier, the U.N. delegate to Leopoldville. However, Lumumba argues that he will give his speech not as president of the National Congo Movement but as prime minister of the Republic of the Congo. He challenges the soldier, calling him an African "traitor," and defies him to shoot him as he attempts to pass. The soldier prepares to shoot Lumumba but then says, "Come to think of it, no. . . . The Congolese will attend to it themselves" (72). The sanza player's closing remarks, with their interweaving of African story and proverb, provide a poetic and metaphorical setting for the tragedy he sees in the situation, in which it is every man for himself.

In scene 11 Lumumba's house has been occupied by Mokutu's paratroopers. In the ensuing conversation Lumumba embraces a constitutional government and rightfully accuses Mokutu of endangering the tender young republic. Mokutu shows little interest in these questions, however, for he is interested only in letting Lumumba know that he has decided to neutralize the government and to fire both him and Kala.

The scene is key to our understanding of the political geography in which the pan-Africanist Lumumba operates. Africa is like the palm of the right hand extended forward; the Congo is the hollow of that hand. Lumumba speaks of Angola, under Portuguese rule in 1960, at the time of the play's action, and still so in 1967, when it was written. Angola, as Lumumba points out, is caught in the vice of slavery owing to its badly recompensed hard labor. He describes San Tomé as a virtual penal colony. He then turns to the evils visited by French, British, and Belgian colonists on Senegal, Mali, Guinea, Cameroun,

Togoland, Ghana, and Dahomey. In short, he brings together here the African struggles for freedom on many fronts. His vision is broad and his longing crosses borders. Mokutu, however, refuses to accept responsibility for the whole of Africa; he will only answer for the Congo, where he "mean[s] to restore order" (76).

Act 3

In the first scene we find our hero imprisoned at Camp Hardy in Thysville with his comrades Mpolo and Okito. Lumumba awakens from a terrible dream. He confesses that there is wisdom even in nightmares. Unlike Lumumba, Mpolo and Okito reject traditional animism and ancestor worship. In a streak of optimism, Lumumba tells his friends that he believes that the waste, disorder, anarchy, corruption, and humiliation are going to cease soon and that "they" will come begging him to take the reins again. He regrets nothing he has done. Still optimistic and certainly in his usual visionary frame of mind, he claims that the struggle has not been just for themselves, not even just for Africans, but for all humankind, the erect species. Lumumba then initiates a conversation with his jailers, in which he explains to them that the money from the national treasury is in Katanga, in Tzumbi's treasury. (He means that the Katanga police have stolen the money; on another level, however, the province of Katanga was vital to the Congolese economy and at the time was controlled by an unholy alliance between the Belgian mining interests and local politicians led by Tschombe.)

As they drink beer, Lumumba turns the conversation to the question of tribalism, which has contributed to the clash of ideologies in the Congo and in most of Africa. (The resolution of this clash is complicated by the fact that some Africans wish to cling to their tribal values; some are Pan-Africanists, nationalists, and federalists; some want local and regional control and government.) But, more importantly, Lumumba is preoccupied with Mokutu's treachery. As he says, "When I appointed the first black officers, how could I imagine that quicker than lava spurts from a volcano, a new caste would be born, the caste of colonels and new masters, and that those voracious, insatiable dogs[13] would monopolize all the benefits of Congolese freedom?" (81). The jailers, moved by Lumumba's discourse, free him in hopes that he can do something to help feed them, and, swearing allegiance to Lumumba, they vow to cut Mokutu's gizzard out if they find him.

Scene 2 serves as a pendant to scene 2 of act 2: it takes place in the African bar, with Mama Makosi speaking to Lumumba, accompanied by Mpolo and Okito. They are speaking of Lumumba's having been betrayed by Mokutu and Kala. Lumumba alludes to the ritual tribal dance of the 12 masks and applies the beliefs revolving around that dance to contemporary events, saying that at the end of the dance the spirit of evil was defeated and prosperity restored, as it will be in the case of the Congolese Republic, to which he proposes a toast. Now he is ready to meet the press. But a man in the bar says that the press must know that Lumumba is their king, and the crowd agrees. For to this man and to the crowd Lumumba is the prophet and the messiah.

Here, then, is the negritude concept encountered in the *Cahier:* Lumumba is the messiah of the Good News, the Gospel. It is he who bears the news that slavery and servitude are dead and that the black race is beautiful, strong, and free. Yet Lumumba balks at being called king (as did Christ) and even more so at being considered a messiah. He says he is no Simon Kibangu, who in the 1930s and 1940s founded a religious movement based on the teachings of the British Baptists, and who was ultimately imprisoned. Kibangu was considered a prophet, and his followers claimed that he, like Christ, had been resurrected. If Kibangu tried to win God back from the white man, he was in error, says Lumumba, for the white man robbed the Africans of much more than God: he robbed them of Africa. Now Africa is hungry to be itself again. For this reason, Lumumba says, he is no messiah.

Pauline's entrance here is again very touching. The further Lumumba travels down his mystic road of sacrifice, the more Pauline pleads with him to remember his wife, his wedding day, his children. She does not want to be a widow. But our hero is intent on his duty. The press now enters, and Lumumba asks them to inform the world of his peaceful intentions: this policy of peace is his foreign policy, and he expects all foreign governments to respond in kind. Of course, Lumumba does not recognize that he has been deposed; he speaks with the voice of authority, as prime minister of the Congo, whose full independence and sovereignty he intends to preserve.

But the paratroopers have arrived during this press conference and surround his house. He knows now that he must die, but he wants no bloodshed, for, says he, "justice cannot be won by violence" (88). Rather, he wishes to die like Gandhi. The paratroopers, with Kala and Mokutu, are allowed to enter, while the press and others are ushered out. Kala asks for Lumumba to capitulate as a leader, but Lumumba refuses. "Mr. President," he says, "I will not be your Quizling. . . . I will not, by my presence [in the Cabinet position you have offered me as a bribe] lend support to a policy that I disavow. And still less will I sponsor a government of corrupt traitors" (90). But Mokutu swears to take this stubborn Lumumba down a peg. The die is cast.

Scene 3 takes us to Elisabethville, the seat of the Katanga government. While drinking copiously, these leaders converse with Mokutu. (Tzumbi and Mokutu, especially, are negotiating together.) Mokutu seeks an agreement from Tzumbi, whereby Katanga will revert to the Congo nation. Tzumbi will hardly concede to this; his condition is that Lumumba be eliminated as a force in the Congo. He wants Lumumba brought to Katanga. Mokutu finds the fulfillment of this requirement difficult, for Lumumba is popular, and, moreover, world opinion would be against the suppression of democracy. At Tzumbi's urging, Mokutu promises, nonetheless, to try to persuade the Congolese government to honor his proposal. The sanza player closes the scene with a most ominous song, in which the little sparrow hawk is asked to tell us whose blood the sun is drinking.

Scene 4 takes place in New York, at the United Nations. Hammarskjöld is speaking with Matthew Cordelier about transferring Lumumba to Katanga. He knows that Lumumba's life is in danger and senses that Cordelier, while claiming to be neutral, hates Lumumba. Hammarskjöld regrets that he has not kept his eyes open. He vows that he will expose Cordelier's part in this plot against Lumumba and accuses him of being a "murderer of Jesus Christ" (96). Thus, the identification of Lumumba with Christ is made manifest, while Mokutu appears to be a Judas, and Cordelier perhaps a Pontius Pilate. (The United Nations was in fact blamed for Lumumba's death, and rightly so. Thus the United Nations also had a role in this passion – indeed, a principal role.)

Scene 5, the last in the English version of the play, is set in a training camp in Katanga. A white mercenary is on stage, and in front of him is a dummy representing a Negro. (White mercenaries were in fact brought in by Tschombe, who had become prime minister to the new president of Katanga. A crude control had been established, but in 1977 there were more violent uprisings, with insurgents from Katanga [now Shaba] invading Zaire. The situation could not be called stable even in 1990.) The mercenary's role is to shoot at the dummy while abusing it verbally, calling it "swine, baboon, savage, magician, ungrateful bastard, nun raper" (97). The theater then grows dark, and when the lights return the mercenary is on stage with the bodies of Okito and Mpolo. Msiri enters (this occurs in scene 6 of the original version), flings himself at Lumumba, and strikes him in the face. (The strike recalls the buffeting of Christ during His passion.) Msiri accuses Lumumba of practicing magic, but Lumumba assures him that he has but one idea, an invincible idea, an infectious idea. Msiri prods Lumumba with his bayonet and cuts him; he sneers at him, telling him that he, Msiri, is man enough to drink Lumumba's blood and eat his heart. (Again the passion of Christ. Here the Last Supper, in fact, provides the intertext, if not the subtext.) Msiri jeers at Lumumba, telling him he is "living his death," but Lumumba corrects him, saying he is "dying his life" (99). As Lumumba falls, Msiri tells the mercenary to finish him off. The mercenary gives Lumumba the coup de grâce with his revolver.

A series of appearances closes out the play: Pauline recites funereal verses; the sanza player sings of the great god Nzambi; Hammarskjöld – the poet, dreamer, and traitor – reels off verses of lamentation but finally settles for the notion that all this was God's will, which he strives to obey. After Hammarskjöld each person who has had a role in the tragedy – the bankers, Tzumbi, Kala, and Mokutu – proceeds, one by one, to exculpate himself.

After a fade out, light returns (scene 8 in the French version). It is July 1966, Independence Day, and the scene is a public square in Kinsasha. Coffins are paraded forth in a string, one representing the "death of the *Belgian* Congo; the second standing for *daddy's* Congo; the third for tribal conflict" (103). Mokutu, in a leopard skin, is haranguing the crowd, calling Lumumba a martyr, an athlete, a hero. Herein lies the irony, although it is, of course, politically expedient for Mokutu to accept Lumumba as hero and martyr. In the long run, Lumumba is more valuable to Mokutu dead than alive. (Mobutu did in fact take control of the government by military coup, promis-

ing but failing to return the Congo to civilian control. He also backed
the losing faction in Angola. He has many enemies.)

As the curtain falls, the sanza player sings of resurrection: "The
sorgho grows; the bird rises from the ground" (103). He warns the
Congolese that now that they are standing on their own two feet,
that they will have to keep their noses clean. In the French version
the concluding sequence of events differs: for instance, the sanza
player sings his song and *then* the coffins are identified. It has been
said that this final scene concerning Independence Day 1966 had
been added in translation to "bring the play up to date, and to show,
at the end, that it is clearly Mobutu who is in power, following Lumumba's death" (Dunn, 10).

Analysis

One of the notable differences between *Une saison au Congo* and
Christophe is the former's strong polarization with the contrasting
figures of Lumumba and Mokutu. Lumumba is the *dis*-interested
prophet, even though he denies it. He is characterized by his humanity–his love for his wife being an important factor. He is, as
Dunn points out, "great because he sought unity" but also because
he is willing to accept death for pan-Africanism. Indeed, it is very
hard to reconcile this position with that of Benelli, who insists
throughout his book on a Marxist-Brechtian analysis of what he calls
Césaire's three *real* plays (*Et les chiens se taisaient* being for him a
surrealist poem), claiming that Lumumba's idealism, which is based
on French concepts of democracy, has distanced him from the
masses. This cannot possibly be Césaire's concept of Lumumba, for
at many points he demonstrates the leader's popularity with the
people.

In contrast, Mokutu, who, as Césaire says, is no more a puppet
than Lumumba, is nonetheless driven by self-interest and, far more
than Christophe or Lumumba, is a political animal (see Dunn , 10).
Despite these marked differences, the two plays do have in common
their presentation of the feminine argument. Mme Christophe urges
her husband to curb his follies. Pauline Lumumba is like Mme
Christophe, but she is a more sympathetically and fully drawn character. Her role is quite Corneillean, and her situation second only to

her husband's in its tragic dimension. Is it by accident that the scene between her and Patrice recalls a scene in Corneille's *Polyeucte*? I think not. Even Pauline's name furnished Césaire with an intertext, if not a subtext, of which he might not have been aware.

David Dunn believes that both plays present a multifaceted, divided, or split hero: "Both men are compelled to play numerous roles in order to operate in the worlds in which they move. They alienate or separate themselves from their fellow man through an obsession which causes them to lose touch with reality and they experience nihilistic despair when their dreams are frustrated and their goals obstructed" (Dunn, 1). One can readily agree with this premise of their mutual alienation, but the notion that Lumumba exhibits nihilistic despair and loses touch with reality is not so easy to embrace. The role of the West and the treason of Mobutu (as Césaire himself finally came to call it in his 1973 revision) are instrumental in obstructing Lumumba's vision or mission. To see Lumumba as little more than a frustrated-dreamer-turned-nihilist is almost certainly to attenuate the drama's tragic force. Nor is it easy to see Christophe in this light either, for Césaire himself disputes the idea that either Christophe of Lumumba are nihilists (Dunn, 2).

Censorship and the accuracy with which events are communicated is another important issue addressed in this play. Not only does Lumumba initially recognize that the newspapers have distorted his character and intentions, but he later on asks the journalists to paint him and his mission as they really are. Both he and his enemies make (or attempt to make) use of the radio to spread their views, and censorship of the media becomes a very real issue here. The kind of intellectual censorship alluded to in Lumumba's case to some extent mirrors that of the poet and politician Agostinho Neto, who suffered a passion almost as bitter as Lumumba's. The analogy is not an idle one, for Neto, like Césaire and Lumumba, underwent that passion in the name of change, the major thrust of the revolutionary hero.

Newspapers, telephone, and radio figure prominently in the modernity *Une saison* embraces, and this modernity in and of itself sets the play apart from *Christophe*, in which Césaire intended to dramatize an event from the more distant historical past. The use of radio, not only as a means of propaganda but also to provide music in the bar, provides a contrast between the Western box and the live sanza player of African tradition. The presence of the radio also sets up a contrast with the conventional use of tom-toms to send messages from village to village.

Simultaneous with its modernity, however, *Une saison au Congo* has a rather medieval side: it is episodic and almost pageantlike, yet it also has much in common with the plays of Brecht, which are also episodic for that matter. It cannot be an easy play to stage, with shifts in geography and setting, from bar to palace, from Africa to Europe to America, from ground to air. Although the stage directions are not long and complex, the author has a very real sense of how a scene is to appear and often uses action on the forestage to prepare for action to follow when the curtain rises.

The many highly metaphorical references to animals in *Une saison au Congo* are of no small interest. Lilian Pestre de Almeida, in a profound 1976 *Présence africaine* article, discerns in this play a "symbolic bestiary."[14] Without denying the play's *engagement*, Pestre de Almeida looks at it from an exemplary and poetic point of view rather than a political or historical one: characters and continents are associated with different birds and animals, some of which are herbivorous or peace-loving, others of which devour and are ponderous, preying, or death-dealing. Thus, for instance, the heavy and powerful buffalo, made ferocious by the slightest tickle, dangerous when wounded, represents Belgium and Flanders. The bankers are *lupetos*, half-wolf, half-human. The Congolese are split into two categories of animals: some are chthonian, others given to heroic free flight. An analysis such as Pestre de Almeida's needs to be made of *all* Césaire's works, which have something in common with the animal symbols used by Senghor and, when not also derived from voodoo, with totemism. Pestre de Almeida asserts that for Césaire the animal is always superior to man and the vegetable superior to the animal, as is established when Lumumba is transfigured from man to bird to tree, a direction that the Western mind would consider backward. At the close of *Une saison* the crowd cries, "Vive Dipenda and *Uhuru*, Lumumba. The great fallen tree will germinate again" (102).

Une saison au Congo is an outstanding example of black theater; it is as clear-cut a tragedy as any in literature. Like the tragic heroes of Corneille, Lumumba knows of and chooses his catastrophic end when he chooses to undertake a larger mission. Lumumba knows his adversaries are powerful, according to Joppa (170), but he also knows he will defeat them and that, thanks to the power of the Word, all the ills inflicted on his country by the colonizers will be redressed. *Une saison au Congo* is about decolonization, hinting at the postcolonial chaos that precedes ultimate triumph. It studies a historical event of metaphorical proportions, focusing on the martyrdom of a culture hero, a revolutionary, an archetypal figure whose fundamental concern is his people. *Une saison au Congo* is a work of lasting importance and of considerable lyrical beauty.

Chapter Six

Une tempête

Obviously modeled after, and even a subversion of, Shakespeare's *The Tempest*, Césaire's *Une tempête* (1969), an "adaptation for Negro theater," seeks to reorient the colonized Caliban, to free him from the shackles of precivilization Prospero has imposed on him. Island imagery once again prevails, and Prospero and Caliban effectively point up the master-slave dynamic.

Seemingly unknown to most commentators on Césaire's play, Ernest Renan, who in his rationalistic and progressivist *Avenir de la science* (1890) proposes that the man of the people is mindless and must be "cultivated," had illustrated his ideas in the 1878 play *Caliban*. At the beginning of Renan's play Caliban is still revolting against a paternalistic and exploitative Prospero, who had usurped Caliban's island and colonized him. Renan imagines Prospero reestablished on his throne in Milan but accompanied there by Caliban, Ariel, et al. In this new setting Caliban ironically feels even less useful than he did as Prospero's island slave. But he manages to mount a revolt and, as leader of the oppressed people, at first holds that Prospero can be brought down by taking his books away from him. (A Renanian agenda also includes forcing Prospero to become a monk!)

Once the Caliban of Renan's play becomes a leader, he is still not respected by Prospero, who hotly points out that Caliban was "never a Christian" and only "aped religion."[1] He claims that Caliban was servant to Setepos, was "garbage," was sensitive only to blows. Now the new duke of Milan, Caliban is, however, accepted by the Church, which calls on him to defend it and also to imprison Prospero. Caliban refuses, however, claiming that Prospero is his protégé, and, having changed his mind about Prospero's books, now wants Prospero to continue his scholarly work under his, Caliban's, patronage.

The essence of Renan's work comes perhaps in act 5, where from the charterhouse prior we learn that if Caliban has made progress, it is only through the laws, morality, and *language* of the aristocracy, that harbinger of civilization. "Inferior races, like the emancipated Negro, at first show a monstrous ingratitude toward those who have civilized them," says the prior. "And when they succeed in shaking off their yoke, these races treat their former superiors as tyrants, exploiters, and imposters. Arch conservatives dream of attempts to get back the power that has escaped them" (Renan, 433; my translation). The close of the play suggests that Prospero may even have the chance to get the reigns of government back from Caliban, and this notion is confirmed by Renan's strange sequel to *Caliban, L'Eau de Jouvence* (1881). In the preface to *L'Eau de Jouvence* Renan sees Prospero as "superior reason" (the magician), momentarily deprived of his authority over the inferior parts of humanity.[2] Had Césaire read these two Renan plays? It is hard to say, but they surely do make for some curious countertextual juxtapositions with *Une tempête*.

Renan's plays are a study in the overthrow of the superior master by the inferior slave and of the role civilization plays in progress. But the strong resemblance of the relationship between Caliban and Prospero in *The Tempest* to that between colonized and colonizer was perhaps first proposed by Octave Mannoni and George Lamming, whose theses, found in *La Psychologie de la colonisation* (1950) and *The Pleasure of Exile* (1960), respectively, are discussed by Janheiz Jahn in his *Neo-African Literature* (239-42). In 1971 *Caliban* became the name of an Angolan poetry journal, while the topos is also central to Liberian Lemuel Johnson's poetry collection *High Life for Caliban*. Johnson writes of "Caliban Agonistes" (Caliban in combat) and offers us ideas revolving around the relationship of the two kinds of men that would not otherwise come readily to mind. He sees Christophe as a type of Caliban who has stumbled onto power. "Sometimes," he writes, "indeed often, we must chew off our legs to escape."[3] Indeed an irony, for this is Caliban's only way of taking revenge on the Prospero who has removed from Caliban his very dream of revenge, at least temporarily.

Nevertheless, the archetypal symbolism of Césaire's characters continues in *Une tempête*. Although this play is not grounded in specific history, its allegorical characters, like those of *Et les chiens se taisaient*, can well represent historical as well as mythological "culture heroes." It has been said that Le Rebelle of *Et les chiens* is, even if accidentally, a black Prometheus Bound in the Aeschylian mold (and Le Promoteur of the same play a white one). I would compare Le Rebelle to Toussaint and Christophe, while Michel Benamou (1974, 7) finds that Ariel of *Une tempête* is a type of Martin Luther King, and Caliban one of Malcolm X. Of course, we need not insist on the translation of these metaphors into concrete historical figures in order to follow the design of or to appreciate the spectrum of human types displayed in *Une tempête*, a substantially less hermetic piece than *Et les chiens se taisaient*. Severely criticizing Harris's omission of the play from his analysis of Césaire's humanism, Christophe Dailly finds that in *Une tempête* "there lies buried an inexhaustible source or spring of human feelings."[4]

Act 1

Uhuru, Swahili for "freedom," was the watchword of the Mau Mau rebellions in Kenya as early as the 1940s. The people shout this slogan to the memory of Lumumba at the end of *Une saison au Congo*. It is Caliban's cry too. Scene 1 is set, poetically speaking, by a discussion of the "storm."[5] The noble captain Antonio Gonzalo senses the need to find a bit of calm in this fierce windy storm. They must land, but the island they sight just before they sink is on fire (hell?). At the end of scene 2 Miranda is calling her father, Prospero, to rescue the sinking ship. He assures her that there is no need to worry and then explains how they, of noble lineage, came to be moored on this island. The Neapolitan king Alonso, Prospero's political rival, and Prospero's younger brother, Antonio, the duke of Milan, had conspired against him by denouncing him to the Inquisition as a magician and sorcerer.

By flashback we have the Inquisitor's title-stripping accusation and arrest of Prospero. Prospero tells Miranda that his trial never took place, but that instead he was abandoned, with her, on this deserted island, which Gonzalo, the king's counselor, had made habitable by providing goods, clothes, books, and instruments. Now the conspirators, avid for new lands to conquer, are about to come ashore. Prospero and Ariel have therefore raised the storm to pre-

vent the landing. Ariel arrives and announces that the mission is accomplished, but he is troubled by the sinking of "that great ship full
of life" (22). He would like to be "freed" from having to do this kind
of work. Prospero tells him he will have his freedom in due course.
Meanwhile, he will have a word or two with "Sir Caliban," who is
getting a little too emancipated.

Prospero summons Caliban, who enters uttering "*Uhuru!*" in
what Prospero terms his "barbaric language." Caliban hurls insults
on Prospero, who reminds the "ugly" monster that it is he, Prospero,
who has taught the stupid brute Caliban to speak. Caliban retorts
that if this is true, it has only been done so that he could carry out
Prospero's orders. He has never taught him "science." And, besides,
without Prospero, Caliban would be king of the island, his island,
which he has inherited from Sycorax, his Mother Earth.

Caliban's animist perspectives prevail as he expresses hostility at
having been cajoled into teaching Prospero the secrets of the island
only to be ghettoized in his grotto and then rejected. Prospero
charges that Caliban tried to rape Miranda, which Caliban denies.
Prospero wants Caliban to help him prepare for the guests he expects "today." Any balking, he warns, and it will be "la trique." Caliban says he will no longer answer to the imposed name "Caliban"
but will from now on be called "X," the "nameless man," the man
who has been robbed of his real name.

Caliban exits, and Prospero tells Ariel that he now recognizes
Caliban to be the real enemy. The shipwrecked passengers are, after
all, "of his race" and are not to be harmed. In fact, Prospero dreams
of a union between Miranda and Alonso's son Ferdinand. Interestingly enough, Prospero realizes that those alliances will help protect
him against the revolutionary Caliban. Ariel begins to sing, which
awakens Ferdinand, who opens his eyes on the beautiful Miranda
and immediately falls in love. Miranda promises to show Ferdinand
all the beauties of the island, but Prospero interrupts. He finds Ferdinand to be an imposter and promises to enslave him, for he is
short of help.

Act 2

Scene 1 shifts the action to Caliban's cave. Ariel has come to warn Caliban of Prospero's plans. Ariel's strategy is to manipulate Prospero nonviolently to try to change him, but Caliban believes Prospero is without conscience and is therefore in need of radical consciousness-raising. Ariel agrees: we must work for the liberation of all, says he. For Prospero this liberation will come in the form of a birth of conscience. Ariel (Martin Luther King?) has always had the dream that the three of them would build a better world. Caliban (Malcolm X?) is very skeptical that fraternity is possible with such a crooked type as Prospero.

In scene 2 Gonzalo and Sebastien discuss the beauties of the island. Gonzalo intends to explore it grotto by grotto, in search of guano, but he also intends to colonize, while not civilizing, any humans he may find. Meanwhile, spirits of the island, directed by an invisible Prospero, lay a table of food before Gonzalo, Sebastien, and Alonso. Just as they are about to eat, the spirits return and carry off the table. They then return with the meal. Prospero goads the spirits, with Ariel as their leader, to continue to torment the three men. This tyrant wants the shipwrecked king and his courtiers "eating from his hand" as a "sign of their submission" (43) and a measure of his power. The three men eat; Alonso laments his "lost son" (44). He and Gonzalo then fall asleep.

At the beginning of scene 3 Antonio enters. To Sebastien he expresses his indignation that the king should be sleeping rather than keeping watch over his flock. In fact, this state invites sedition: "It is time to shake the royal coconut tree. . . . And when one shakes a tree, someone must fall" (46). They are about to kill Alonso and Gonzalo when Ariel awakens the sleeping pair, informs them of the mounting conspiracy, and tells them that he, Ariel, is sent by Prospero, who rules over the island and who will save them, since they repent sincerely of their past evil deeds.

Act 3

In scene 1, which is twice as long as the two remaining scenes, Ferdinand digs in the soil as he sings the song of a forced laborer. Caliban looks on in envy. All he can sing is "ouende, ouende, ouende, macaya" (53; an African-American song encouraging slaves to eat more). He has no pretty girl to comfort him. Miranda speaks to Ferdinand, and Caliban whispers her name to Ferdinand, but Prospero enters and the young man quickly returns to his work. Prospero tells Caliban to take over Ferdinand's work. Caliban balks, but does it. It begins to rain. Says Caliban, "Patience, I'll get them yet" (56). Caliban's "patience" reminds us of Sartre's list of the qualities of the Negro race. The idea of being "long-suffering" and of lying in wait for the right moment to rebel is repeatedly expressed in negritude poetry. It is the backdrop for Léon-Gontran Damas's "Bientôt" and feeds an important passage of the *Cahier* in which Césaire defines his negritude as, in part, a "droite patience." (The word *patience* is etymologically tied to the word *passion*, or suffering, as well.) Caliban, Le Rebelle reincarnate, curses, "Let the seven maws of Malediction bark!" (56).

In a somewhat Rabelaisian scene 2 we meet Trinculo as he prepares for a voyage. Caliban enters; Trinculo thinks of capturing him and exhibiting him at a fair in Europe. (Here we have shades of Renaissance explorers who brought New World inhabitants back to Europe as "specimens" and of explorers to Africa who brought native peoples and animals – and peoples as animals – back to Europe as exotic and uncivilized examples of African fauna.) For the time being, Trinculo simply takes refuge from the rain with Caliban.

Stephano enters drinking and singing a whaling song. Seeing Caliban, he, like Trinculo, takes him for an Indian and imagines he has caught him and will exhibit him in a European freak show. He then spots Trinculo, who he takes for Caliban's Siamese twin. Then Stephano and Trinculo recognize each other. Stephano proposes to "civilize" Caliban just enough so that Caliban can help them, and so that they can exploit him. Stephano pours drink into Caliban's mouth to make him talk. (Alcoholism was the white man's "gift" to Indians and blacks. The practice is alluded to at the beginning of *Une saison au Congo*.)

Meanwhile, Stephano and Trinculo imagine taking over the island, since the king and the duke are probably both dead, but they dispute which one shall have the crown. Stephano declares himself king, after Caliban proclaims it, and he names Trinculo "Maréchal." However, Caliban warns Stephano of the "usurper" Prospero, who has seized the island from him, Caliban, the rightful owner. Stephano and Trinculo propose to do away with Prospero, and so Caliban will have his vengeance, or so Caliban thinks. He sings a song to liberty. But Stephano, too drunk to act until the morrow, falls into a deep sleep.

Scene 3 shifts to Prospero's grotto. Here we see Prospero as a theater director, a *metteur en scène*, much like Alcandre, the magician-director of Corneille's *Illusion comique*. He wants to stage a *divertissement* for a wedding gift; better, he wants to inculcate in his audience the spectacle of tomorrow's world, full of reason, beauty, and harmony. Although generally Caliban, not Prospero, is Césaire's *porte-parole*, in this particular instance we recall Césaire's own dramatic goal: to divert and to instruct, which seems derived, like that of Alcandre and Prospero, from classical doctrine. (The dramatic goal of Prospero may, on the other hand, ironically call up the white man's flawed concepts of reason, beauty, and harmony rather than Césaire's aesthetic.)

One by one, Prospero conjures up the gods and goddesses of the Romans; Juno, Ceres, Iris, and then Eshu, the evil one. He wonders if Ariel has made a mistake and if his magic is slipping. But Eshu explains that even though he had not been invited, he came anyway. Prospero tells him to leave, and Eshu agrees, but only after singing a priapic song in honor of the wedding party. The gods leave. Prospero calls on Ariel to subdue and punish Caliban, who continues his guerrilla campaign against him; Ariel suggests that Prospero attempt to understand and indulge Caliban, who is a rebel. Prospero, however, wants Caliban's insubordination punished. He suggest Ariel subdue him with glass beads and other trinkets of the sort that savages are inclined to adore.

Through part-voodoo, part-Creole incantations scene 4 evokes the spirits of the tropical forest: fly, ant, *charognard* (buzzard), crab, hummingbird. Caliban awakens, mobilizes this group that has been directed against him, and advances singing his war song to Shango. (According to Owusu-Sarpong [124], Shango is a Yoruba god of thunder who appears in the Antilles, Africa, Brazil, and the United States.) Caliban then meets Stephano, to whom he explains that he has nature (sea, wind) on his side; to Trinculo he explains that the discomforts he is experiencing (from sun, rain, mud, and mosquitoes) are not the products of nature but "inventions" of

Prospero "to render people stupid, to blind them, to make them sneeze, and to make them weep" (77).

Seeing that Prospero will not be easy to deal with, Stephano decides to have a fortifying drink or two, after which he and Trinculo again fall into competitive quarrelling and then into combat. Caliban sees he will have to fight his battle with Prospero alone. And in fact Prospero has just come on the stage. Caliban is about to beat Prospero but then thinks better of it. The three rebels are taken prisoner by Ariel, at Prospero's behest.

In scene 5, at Prospero's grotto, Ferdinand and Miranda are playing chess. Alonso enters with Gonzalo; they heap blessings on the couple. Prospero enters and, after telling them all to rest – for tomorrow they will all set sail for Europe – he sets Ariel free.

Stephano, Trinculo, and Caliban enter; Stephano and Trinculo "explain" themselves and are pardoned. Prospero then tells them to store up their drink, for "tomorrow we set sail." All that is left is for Caliban to defend himself and be pardoned. But Caliban has only one regret: that he has failed to get back his island and regain his freedom. If only he could get back his island he would purge it of all trace of Prospero. (Again the theme of the corruption of the island paradise by the European settler [colonizer] is in play. In essence, Caliban is longing for the catharsis that would come with ridding his island of the marks of Western civilization.)

Here, again like Le Rebelle, Caliban rehearses the long list of humiliations and tortures he has suffered under Prospero's tyrannical reign. But, says he, "now I don't give a hang about you, your power, *your dogs*, your police, your inventions . . . because I know that one day I'll get you, impaled on your own stake" (88).

The speech in which Caliban rejects the image of himself as sub-human and inferior to the white man is vintage Césaire and links *Une tempête* to the preceding plays and poems, especially to *Et les chiens se taisaient*. Caliban finishes his tirade with the "vocation," which is really nothing more than to foul up Caliban's life.

But the profoundest level of Prospero's lack of humanism comes through his ironic response: "Of the brute, of the monster I made [a] man. But oh! To have failed to find the path to the heart of man" (90). He adds in a voice not that of Césaire, "If indeed that is man." (Prospero is not convinced of Caliban's humanity; such doubt continues to lurk in the minds of many whites.) Prospero then bids

farewell to his friends, for, as Caliban has predicted, he will remain
on the island, fighting "violence with violence."

Analysis

One somehow feels that the racial conflicts this play depicts are
thought of by its author as being of a permanent nature. Although
some (Soyinka, Condé, Boukman) have criticized the "optimism" of
negritude, that supposed optimism seems seriously absent from *Une
tempête*. Even the title, with its indefinite article, suggests that the
storm of the play is but a segment in a saga of ongoing strife rather
than an event in which a major, decisive uprising occurs and substantially changes the "climate" or "atmosphere." For until Caliban
"someday" with his long patience "gets" Prospero – and this is projected to an undesignated point in the future – there will be many a
violent confrontation. The racist Prospero seems not to change; he
regards Caliban's very speech, or language, as "barbaric." (How often have we heard this said of African languages, so readily referred
to as dialects or "lingo" or "mumbo jumbo"?) Prospero not only de-
grades Caliban by these devaluating attitudes but in the end questions his very humanity.

Césaire makes it clear that Prospero's assumptions about Caliban's speech are from one end to the other fundamentally false.
Prospero assumes to have taught Caliban language/speech and
therefore to have "civilized" him. But the fact that Caliban expresses
his deepest longings in Swahili reveals a pre-Prospero gift of
language and is one of the best clues that an authentic African culture informs Caliban with a background to be envied. These facts re-
focus the Prospero-Caliban relationship. Even if it is somewhat difficult to see Prospero as an American, we are in the presence here not
just of a teacher-student or master-slave dynamic but of a newly
awakened but long-since-sophisticated conscience in revolt against
the evils of a colonization. Thus, in time, through rebellion and revolution, the old philosophy, the old body politic represented by
Caliban, the vox populi, may indeed once again overtake and replace
Prospero's autocratic, unworkable, and destructive policy.

Assuming that Caliban, as a part of nature, is inferior to Prospero
is as false as assuming that Prospero has given Caliban language. He

has not given him language but, like all colonizers, has forced on him a language. Corzani sees a role reversal in the play: Caliban becomes an authentic man; he is never inferior, in fact, but only made to feel and seem so. As Jahn says, "Once Caliban has recognized the limits and roots of Prospero's power, he may try some further unsuccessful revolts; but if his urge to freedom remains unbroken, the idea is bound to occur to him in the end . . . that his mother's powers, the voices, the instruments and the riches that drop in dreams, all belong together . . . that they form a culture, but one very different from Prospero's book culture" (Jahn 1968b, 241). Jahn is mistaken, however, to say that Caliban has no other language than Prospero's to do this with. He has his own; he *also* has Prospero's, which he may use and turn against him, just as the negritude poets intended to do with French. Within the terms of this process Prospero will have to relearn his own refashioned language from an ironic, even cynical, Caliban, who was "civilized" long before the fact of the white man's historical arrival on the African scene.

Une tempête is a lucid and complex dramatization of many political postulations. The various characters reflect many social strata so that the play is also the dramatization of prevailing socioeconomic conditions. Caliban, the blackest, is the most subjected; he has a great many rungs to climb on any ladder before he can call himself the equal of Prospero. Prospero's position of colonial-style domination is the most tenuous. Already he has been deposed as duke of Milan and now faces new rivalry from other nobles, Alonso and Antonio, who would, like the stream of white colonizers who succeeded one another in the Antilles, replace his rule. Added to this, and even more fundamental, are the interior threats to his regime: the intellectual mulatto Ariel and the Negro Caliban. Ariel is tired of serving Prospero; Caliban, who, like Prospero, is deposed, is in outright revolt against Prospero's subjugation and will form coalitions if necessary. Desperate for reform, he will have recourse to violence.

Caliban's revolution fails in part because he has formed dangerous and unfruitful alliances with Trinculo and Stephano, two drunken wastrels. He slowly comes to realize that he must fight his battles alone, a position we have seen in all Césaire's preceding works.

Césaire's Ferdinand and Miranda tell us something about love. In Shakespeare's play, the forces of love win out. In Césaire's so-called Negro adaptation love, at least in the white world, is a sham. Ferdinand would cheat at cards with his bride-to-be. This says in shorthand what we may expect of him as future husband and citizen. And romantic love in the black world is not depicted here. Indeed, it is seldom a topic with Césaire, although in works such as *Christophe* we have found the black woman counseling moderation and compromise. In this play it is as if the colonized woman has been overlooked, except as a metaphor for Mother Earth, for nature, Caliban's genetrix whom he certainly does not forget. By and through her we may one day see the rebirth of man against a collapsing background.

It would seem that collapse and the subsequent rebirth must be violent, for Prospero, though he is losing, does not give up easily, and he is prepared, as he says at the end of the play, to fight violence with violence. He is, as Owusu-Sarpong has put it, "a wicked colonist who needs his knowledge and his repressive arsenal to assure order" (120). But he is more. He will descend to disorder, even chaos. In Prospero's polis the colonist is far more dependent on the colonized – Ariel, Caliban, and Ferdinand – than they are on him. This central irony, only hinted at by Owusu-Sarpong (122-25), suggests that the ultimate collapse of Prospero's "system" is not far off. The irony of dependency also recalls chief pieces of twentieth-century literature, such as Jean Genet's *The Maids* or *The Blacks*, in which the master-slave dynamic is in some sense reversed. Prospero has no friends; Prospero believes he needs no friends. As the people of Binga would have it, "He who walks down the road alone will be swept away by the river."

Chapter Seven

Essays

Susan Frutkin has referred to Césaire's discursive works as those of maturity and of expanding visions. But in choosing to express his visions in the essay form as well as in verse and drama, Césaire is using the same process as such artists as Jorge Luis Borges, Léopold Senghor, T. S. Eliot, and George Santayana, who kept journals and wrote philosophical and theoretical prose that illuminated their artistic product. In Césaire's essays, which have their own paraliterary value, we find the same themes of anticolonialism, decolonization, and revolution found in his poems and plays. We also find the exploration of the nature of the black martyr and culture hero (here Toussaint Louverture) and a profound probing of Marxist communism and fascism. We find the same criticisms of Western capitalist societies and of the hypocrisies visited on the black world by so-called Christians.

Discours sur le colonialisme

The earliest prose essays come in the journal *Tropiques*, where, above all, the ills of the Vichy government are exposed. In 1950 we have the all-important *Discours sur le colonialisme* in which Césaire shows the vast difference between colonization and civilization, contending that one negates the other. (To put one civilization in contact with another would be good, he concedes, but the question is, "Has colonization really allowed for contact?")[1] Here too we encounter the poet's contempt for Europe – its rationalism and pseudohumanism that have allowed it to mount one of the most devastating holocausts in human history. Moreover, the colonizeds' realization of these flaws in the Western structures helps to establish the fact that the colonized from now on have the advantage over their "masters" (*Discours*, 8). This essay's most potent message may be

Césaire's excoriation of fascism and the master-slave or colonial
mentality of Nazism. In a rather famous passage, Césaire claims that
the whites' horror over the Holocaust is racially based and that the
demon Hitler dwells in the heart of every white man:

> It would be worthwhile to study, clinically, and in detail, the procedures of
> Hitler and of Hitlerism, and to bring out to the all too distinguished, all too
> humanistic, all too Christian bourgeois of the twentieth century that he bears
> within himself a Hitler of which he is unaware; that Hitler inhabits him, that
> Hitler is his demon, and that it is not logical that he should grow vituperative,
> that at bottom what he does not pardon Hitler for is not the crime itself, but
> that the crime was against the white man; what he does not pardon is not the
> crime in and of itself, but the humiliation of the white man, and for having
> applied, in Europe, colonialist procedures up until then visited only upon
> such peoples as the Arabs of Algeria, the coolies of India and the negroes of
> Africa. (*Discours*, 12-13; my translation)

Nazism is at bottom merely another manifestation of racism, another kind of colonialization, says Césaire, and, what is more, long
before Hitler there were Hitlers, speaking through the mouths of so-
called humanists. The French conquests of Algeria and Vietnam fall
under the category of colonization as well, despite hypocritical rationalization regarding occupation and concurrent massacres
(*Discours*, 16-17). Colonization dehumanizes rather than carries out,
as the colonizers claim, the mission of "humanism" (*Discours*, 18).
The loss by colonization of such great civilizations as the Aztec and
the Incan is inconsolable, the more so because Césaire can see
nothing of any value brought to the people in the place of its civilization but "hard labor, intimidation, pressure, police, taxes, robbery,
rape, compulsory cultures, scorn, mistrust, . . . mindless elites and
masses brought low" (*Discours*, 19). He argues that there has been
no progress but that, rather, cultures have been crushed, religions
stamped out, artistic masterpieces annihilated, extraordinary potential suppressed. To an argument that agriculture has improved, he
responds saying that viable, harmonious economies have been undermined, only to be replaced by an agriculture oriented toward the
benefit of the Metropole.

In the times before colonization, says Césaire, there were *communities* ruled by authentic democratic systems. But true democra-
cies no longer exist. Africa was destroyed when it fell into the hands

of a Europe that had just fallen into the hands of the most un-
scrupulous financiers and industrialists. Now colonial Europe has
piled modern abuse on ancient injustice, odious racism on an old
inequality in which European explorers refused to recognize peoples
of Africa and the New World as their brothers ("leurs semblables")
in either body or spirit (*Discours*, 24-26). Arguments for slavery and
racist views were thus facilitated and are found in abun-
dance – spiritual arguments as early as Joseph de Maistre, or scientific
arguments in such writings as those of [Georges Vacher de] Lapouge.
Quote follows quote, from [Ernest] Psichari, [Emile] Faguet, and
Jules Romains. Arguments for the great Benin bronzes and for
African music follow.

But the racism persists despite these proofs of African grandeur
and even despite the great writer Leo Frobenius's proclamation that
"the idea of the Negro as barbaric is a European invention" (quoted
in *Discours*, 30). The bourgeois plug their ears, however. They may
argue that all is done in "good faith," but Césaire responds that
"their subjective good faith has no relationship to the objective and
the social impact of the bad job they are doing as guard-dogs of the
'colonialisms'" (*Discours*, 32).

Racist passages are quoted again, this time from [Pierre] Gourou
(*Les Pays tropicaux*) and Father [Placide] Tempels, a Belgian missionary. From these, and from historians, novelists, sociologists, and
psychologists, we have the whole gamut of "good faith" arguments:
primitivism, biased investigations, self-interested generalizations,
chauvinism, false objectivity. Gourou and Tempels are particularly
ridiculed, but [Octave] Mannoni, with his monstrous study of the
soul of the Madagascar people, is equally attacked. Doubtless, these
are examples of a widespread justification of fundamentally racist
theories, but they are espoused by the petit bourgeois, who is also
all too willing to accept Yves Florenne's theorizing against the
dilution of pure French blood and the shock of "métissage" in a
manner that shows how France, only five years after Hitler's defeat,
is chewing over his vomit (*Discours*, 41-43). And if that bourgeoisie
perpetuates this racism, injustice, and inequality, it does so out of
fear, for, according to Césaire, it knows in its heart of hearts that it is
about to meet its demise: "it is with its head buried under the
manure that a society sings its swan song" (*Discours*, 43).

In a sense, the next chapter takes a curious turn in a literary direction. Césaire defends *Les Chants de Maldoror* by Lautréamont, one of Césaire's "masters," if we dare use that term in this context. As far as Césaire is concerned, Lautréamont saw clearly what a monster the capitalist society could produce (*Discours*, 45). (Balzac's Vautrin is not unlike Lautréamont's Maldoror, Césaire claims, and Baudelaire's *chiffonnier* (rag picker) is the supreme example of the poor, the people for whom the rich refuse to make a place [*Discours*, 44-46]).[2]

Again Césaire predicts that the bourgeoisie is condemned to take on all the abuses of history – inquisition, war (justified by some *raison d'état*), and racism as a rationalization for enslavement – for it is the bourgeoisie that embodies the ideal of "human progress." The section ends with a most ironic analysis of contemporary ethnologists, including Roger Caillois. While Caillois would argue that the West has produced the great inventions, Césaire recalls that it was the Egyptians who gave the world arithmetic and geometry, the Assyrians who gave astronomy, and the Arabs who gave chemistry. Even though Caillois sees these contributions as incomplete until they are developed by the West, Césaire considers these annexations unacceptable. Moreover, he virtually ridicules Caillois's claims of superiority in the domain of morality and religion, in view of the Westerners' oppression of their Third World brothers.

In the last section Césaire attacks the West's concept of humanism and its notion of *nation*, two values it has invented and thrust on the world – values that have been mere masks for pillage, murder, and servitude. This behavior suggests that Europe will soon perish if it does not take note of the vacuum it has created and is still creating: "No more dams. No more boulevards. The hour of the Barbarian has arrived. The modern Barbarian. The American hour. Violence, lack of discipline, waste, mercantilism, bluff, gregarianism, stupidity, vulgarity, disorder" (*Discours*, 57). Cited as the worst of evils, perhaps, is America's intention to raffle off all the colonies in the world.

In the closing paragraphs of this essay Césaire reveals his now-dated Marxism, identifying the proletariat as those who will execute the revolution and bring about a "classless society," the proletariat being the "only class which still has a universal mission, since it incorporates the suffering of all of history's ills" (*Discours*, 59).

A short essay of 58-some pages, Césaire's *Discours* packs many arguments into its succint paragraphs. According to Hubert Juin, "however powerful it may be, however clear and precise," *Discours sur le colonialisme* is "only a proof–and an almost superfluous one–brought to the real work."³ Was the *Discours* really written for those who "refused" to understand the poetry collections, as Juin hypothesizes? Perhaps. But why not as well say that the *Discours* was written for a different audience, one that does not follow metaphoric language so well as strict discourse? We would have to add, however, that if in the *Discours* Césaire avoids the risk of being misunderstood because of the metaphorical, lyrical language of his poetry, he takes an equally great (if not greater) risk of being misunderstood here because of his heavy use of irony. A reader may well miss the fundamental thrust of many a passage in which Césaire is saying the opposite of what he means. I do not imply, of course, that irony is absent from the *Cahier* and other poems: irony is the mark of all great poems, and is certainly used in many places in the *Cahier*.⁴

Culture, Colonization, and Responsibility

During the First International Congress of Black Writers in 1956, Césaire gave an address entitled "Culture et colonisation" in which he again asserts his concern for the fate of the world's blacks and for that of diverse cultures as they meet with the oppression of colonizers. Indeed, he asserts that the problem of colonization is integrally linked to the fate of these black cultures. He says that political and social repression can only submerge a people's self-determination, along with their culture and creativity. He is vehemently against the imposition of a civilization as a capitalist mode: it is here that he rejects the concept of a "civilisation métisse" (interbreeding of the two civilizations, the colonizing and the colonized). *Integration* is proposed as a preferable model ("Culture," 200). He concludes that such *integrated* types of civilizations are nonexistent (this is in 1956, remember) and that only those that are juxtaposed are visible. This program has amounted to what he calls "cultural anarchy," and in his speech he contends that the only solution to the problem of culture clash is to liberate the colonized and provide them with the opportunity to achieve the synthesis of indigenous and European cultural traits that conforms to their needs. In the long run, he says, a superior civilization might well emerge.

It is not surprising to learn that in his preface to Daniel Guérin's *Les Antilles décolonisées*, also published in 1956, Césaire should continue to advance his theories on a postcolonial policy that would benefit the oppressed.[5] It is departmentalization that he is discussing in "Culture et colonisation," however, and he therefore focuses on the need for the departments of Martinique, Guadeloupe, and French Guyana to participate fully in the spirit of nations that have achieved individuality. According to Césaire, the peoples of this region are undergoing an awakening; their sense of nationality–this embryonic national conscience–must be acknowledged: it will be possible to build a future on the idea of nationality alone (local, not West Indian and not French). This is what Césaire believes Guérin has overlooked. Each little island is to become a nation unto itself, a valid national community, and not, as has been proposed by some, a part of a federation of the Antilles. Susan Frutkin (36) sees these theories as contradictory to Césaire's declared espousal of communism and concludes that already in 1956 his adherence to Marxism could only have been conditional. It was, in fact, in 1956 that Césaire resigned from the French Communist party.

In October 1956 Césaire wrote his famous letter to the leader of the French Communist party, Maurice Thorez, in which he explains his reasons for resigning from the party.[6] Here Césaire decries the horrendous crimes of Stalin that were recently exposed by Khrushchev. Closer to home, however, he denounces the French Communist party for not declaring its independence from the Soviet Union, for its unwillingness to condemn Stalin, and for its self-satisfied, antidemocratic methods. On a more personal level, Césaire seems to sense that the uniqueness of colored people and their problems made their ways and destinies different from those of other races. Césaire concludes that the ways and destinies of colored men and those of communism, at least as it is practiced, are not "identical." He again deals with the question of colonialism while asserting that blacks' struggle against racism is a more pressing one than the struggle of the French worker against management can possibly be. Neither is blacks' struggle to be considered subsidiary to the struggle against capitalism.

Césaire also objects to the fact that communism in Martinique had been subsumed under that of Western Europe, resulting in less attention devoted to the political and social problems germane to the islands and Caribbean in nature. And worst of all, Césaire discerns within the Communist parties of Western Europe an assimilationism and chauvinism – a sense of superiority – that ill accord with the objectives of communism. He concludes by calling for a Marxism and communism that are harnessed to the service of colored peoples and not the reverse and for a "Copernican revolution" amongst Europeans. (Is he saying that the sun does not rise and set in Europe?) He looks not to Europe for regeneration of the Antilles but to black Africa, for although he espouses the concept of the universal, his universal embraces many particulars.

This letter, key to the understanding of Césaire's evolution, is also an important political (even literary) piece dealing with pan-Africanism and ranking, in the words of Colin Legum, as "one of the classical texts of anti-colonialism."[7] It documents the antipathies between the causes of communism and the needs of a postcolonial black population worldwide, but it also provides a text of great conviction and passion by a poet whose commitment abides even as his political vehicles for the execution of that commitment must change.

If Césaire's focus had changed a bit by 1959, his passion did not. At the Second International Congress of Black Writers in Rome that year, he delineated in a speech (published as the paper "L'Homme de culture et ses responsabilités") the responsibilities of the black intellectual. Particularly striking here is that Césaire is looking at what might be done from within the black communities rather than aiming at the failures and duties of European and American imperialists. Césaire insists that decolonization must be truly revolutionary; it will involve the destruction of any prevailing institution that is harmful. One cannot fail to grasp the Marxist nature of the call or to see, with Frutkin (43-44), the paradox of Césaire's position, for at that time Césaire occupied a seat in the National Assembly of France – surely a hallmark of French imperialist establishment and very likely a "harmful" institution.

Toussaint Louverture

In the important study *Toussaint Louverture: La Révolution française et le problème colonial,*[8] Césaire demonstrates his brilliance as archivist and historian. He resumes his considerations of Toussaint, the great revolutionary of Saint-Domingue (Haiti), whom he had shown under poetic colors in the *Cahier.* We know the story: how in the wake of the French Revolution Toussaint led the slaves in revolt against the French monarchy, and, after the French had abolished slavery, sought to become the sole master of the island. He sent the French off, and when the blacks revolted against him, he seized rule of Haiti in 1801. But, tragically, Napoleon envoyed his general, Leclerc, to overtake the island. Toussaint was arrested and deported to Fort-de-Joux in the Jura mountains, where he died.

It is, in fact, Césaire's intention to demonstrate to what an extent the French Revolution failed in colonial milieus, such as that of Haiti. Although the Declaration of the Rights of Man had been promulgated, the mulattoes of Saint-Domingue saw clearly that equality was not forthcoming to them. Robespierre was arguing that granting them this civic independence was tantamount to forcing a schism between them and the whites, and therefore to pushing them into the camp of the blacks, who were threatening insurrection. Were this to happen, the mulattoes would necessarily join in with the blacks. This was, in fact, what happened. And in view of the fact that Marat – who in the eyes of Césaire was the first anticolonialist – had proclaimed the right of the colonies to secession, the revolt, which was nothing short of a civil war, was initiated, with Toussaint as leader of the rebels.

Césaire believes Toussaint was chosen as leader for his firm character and superior intellect. A precious recruit he was, because he was a chief in the stamp of Nestor, or so the rebels believed. He was also a man of tact: "He was able to slip into the slot and take possession of it without alarming anyone" (*Toussaint*, 46; my translation). At 48, his time had come, and he knew it. Under him the budding insurrection became a revolution. This, Césaire tells us, was accomplished by disciplining the revolutionaries and raising their military and political levels, and, in particular, by making them conscious of the fact that it was not men that they had to destroy but a system.

Step by step, Césaire recounts how Toussaint became "the first great anticolonial leader that history has known" (*Toussaint*, 48). That he carried out this revolution on Haitian soil as a phenomenon of his own political strategies, knowing that the colony had need of a "tête politique" (*Toussaint*, 48), is a salient feature of the event. Toussaint recognized that he was the one to be this "tête." Helped by his lieutenant Dessalines, he puts Villatte to flight. He reinstalls the ousted white governor Laveaux, who takes him as adjoint, or vice governor.

Some have accused Toussaint of ambition, but not Césaire: Toussaint was swept on by the force of events and by historic thrust, on which he had his eye riveted. He all too readily realized, for example, that the French were about to renege on their promise to abolish slavery, and that each day the situation worsened. In the beginning, Toussaint had leaned on the blacks and on the representatives of France, and against the white colonists and the mulattoes, but he now saw that it was time to mount a coup against the Metropole. Ironically, to achieve this goal, he turned to his former enemies, the mulattoes. He sent Sonthonax back to France and prepared for the rupture with the Metropole. This expulsion of the divisive Sonthonax rallied the mulattoes around him as never before.

The French, then, sent Hédouville to replace Sonthonax, and the first task of the new French emissary was to attempt to reduce Toussaint's power and to crush the alliance of blacks and mulattoes, which he saw to be in operation. Toussaint pursued his course and in 1798 mobilized Haiti's blacks – a mobilization at once military and spiritual, but also economic. He urged the blacks to work: to export, to cultivate in order to export. For this mobilization he also needed experts. But where to find them? For this he turned to the white colonists. Some have referred to this as a pro-white policy, but not Césaire: Toussaint was not pro-white, but the profoundest of exigencies required him to use the whites in his mission. He preached not only work but also discipline (not unlike Lenin or Christophe).

Unfortunately, writes Césaire, if Toussaint's ideas were good, his methods were less so. His failure, says our poet and essayist, was due to his too great reliance upon military strategies to accomplish his ends and to solve all his problems. And when General Leclerc, at Napoleon's behest, finally marched on Toussaint's forces, it was open warfare.

Meanwhile, Christophe, who in the future was to become the king, was obliged to surrender at Ennery. For Toussaint, this was the fatal blow. When Christophe passed under the authority of Leclerc, Toussaint was, as it were, obliged to cease fire. A political, not a military failure, says Césaire. Toussaint had not sufficiently revealed the persons behind the masks that were to prove ultimately to be the enemies: the masses were still "mystified" by Leclerc, who led them to believe that he held freedom and equality for blacks as a sacred right. Against this, Toussaint's counter propaganda was indeed "poor." Notable is the fact that, for some reason, he never pronounced the magic word "independence." Perhaps he judged it too premature. His strategies proved outdated and "sclerotic," and the consequences were grave.

Although he sought to hold on to two strategic points, the ports of Saint-Marc and L'Arcahaye, and to preserve his army intact, Toussaint accepted General Brunet's invitation. Knowing that it was a "rendezvous with death" (*Toussaint*, 54), even so, he did not decline. For Césaire, the act of acceptance was at once a political and mystical act. Toussaint knew it was a trap, yet he would go. And the tragedy followed. Césaire suggests that we might explain Toussaint's behavior from a psychological angle: Toussaint had a tragic sense of life. A Christian and a contemporary of the French Revolution, he envisioned, as did others of his contemporaries, a modern form of destiny. He may have proposed to die like other "revolutionary martyrs" such as Danton or Robespierre. Whatever his reasons, and perhaps they included his realization that it was time for him to disappear–both because the island was slowly gaining its freedom and because his "disappearance" would provide the necessary pause for this end–he walked to exile and death with his eyes wide open.

At this point Césaire quotes at length from Toussaint's own account of the rendezvous with Brunet and then "evokes" a dialogue that Toussaint had as he boarded the ship (ironically called *Le Héros*) with the ship's commander, Savari. The image of the tree, which we have encountered in several of Césaire's works, is put into the mouth of Toussaint, who says, "In toppling me, they have only leveled the trunk of the tree of black liberty in Saint-Domingue; it will grow up again, from the roots, because they are deep and many" (*Toussaint*, 55).

It is through the accounts of Baille, the jailer at Fort-de-Joux, that we learn of Toussaint's passion. By lengthy quotations, Césaire gives us a description of the tiny dungeon cell in which Toussaint was kept – doors bolted, closely guarded. Baille is told, among other things, to remove all possessions from Toussaint, including his watch, and his uniform. A general, Toussaint was denied the dignity that ought to have been accorded a military prisoner. Rather, Baille was told that Toussaint, for his hideous conduct and his tyranny against the Europeans, deserved nothing but the deepest scorn for his ridiculous pride.

As for Toussaint's death, preceded by a short illness, Césaire quotes here from an administrative report made by the chief of battalion Amiot, in the driest and most documentary style. The crispness in the detailing of events, rattled off in a detached manner, renders the account all the more painful. But the final paragraphs of this strongly committed version of history turn the Amiot passage around. Césaire recapitulates the events: in one page he reiterates the name "Toussaint" (alternating it with "Toussaint Louverture") six or seven times, so as to demonstrate that he was central to this story of Haiti's revolt against its oppressors, and that "Saint-Domingue" is not really castrated by the death of Toussaint – a scapegoat, as was Lumumba – for "the tree indeed had many deep and numerous roots" (*Toussaint*, 58). The independence of Haiti's blacks and people of color was proclaimed at Fort-Dauphin in 1803, and the proclamation's promulgators swore never to give in to any power on earth. (But, although Césaire does not say so, by 1804 the French sent an expedition to Haiti to restore the institution of slavery on the island.)

As far as the portrait of Toussaint Louverture's calvary is concerned, both this study and the *Cahier* deal with Césaire's conceptualization of the evil of colonization. Both deal with what he considers to be a willful postponement of decolonization, and both delineate Césaire's views of racism, paternalism, greed, and treachery. They are, of course, different from one another in approach. Frutkin sees in the essay a "mellowed Césaire" (46) and, moreover, makes much of the fact that the essay offers proof of Césaire's debt to his French "heritage." (Might one not better have said his "education"? After all, a black citizen of Martinique does not, strictly speaking, have a French heritage.) Frutkin's appreciation may amount to an oversimplification: that the style is subdued – as a historical study should be – and that the use of irony is diminished may be one thing, but that the bitterness and the tone of reproach are still not absent from the essay is quite another.

On Aesthetics

Of Césaire's influential writings on aesthetics, "Poésie et connaissance," first given as a speech in Haiti on 28 September 1944 and eventually published in *Tropiques* in January 1945, stands out. Here Césaire states his seven *propositions poétiques* and advances his thesis that poetry replenishes knowledge because the poet can summon up everything that ever was, is, or will be possible. He endorses Breton's concept that poetry is the flag of imagination. Indeed, an image is, he maintains, a "miraculous weapon." Poetry itself is insurrectional, he holds, for poetry reframes language. He argues that the world must return to its original chaos, order must revert to disorder, and in this, as Clayton Eshleman correctly points out in his preface to *Aimé Césaire: The Collected Poetry*, we see how Césaire is the "soul mate" of Sade, Laclos, and Bataille. Perhaps most strikingly, Césaire here asserts that the music of poetry comes from a point beyond sound, from a place more distant than music. As an extension of this essay, and of Césaire's views on the "music of poetry," we should restate the function of rhythm in Césaire's poetry, instrumental in evoking African tom-toms, dance, and voodoo. We should also recall the manner in which our poet has managed to reshape the French language, as observed by Sartre in "Orphée noir." Above all, we should note how Césaire intends to use speech beyond music, beyond intellectual content as a point of his program. He makes powerful and effective use not only of rhythms but of repetitions, accelerations, pauses, and stops. In his verse, lyricism, epic grandeur, and dramatic compression converge. One has the quiet tones as from the caldera of a silent volcano, followed by explosions that terminate in orgasmic or, as Eshleman puts it, climactic upheaval. One might also say that some of Césaire's verse impacts with magnum force and effect.

Césaire says he always wanted to "bend" French (somewhat like Mallarmé): "I re-create a language that is not French," he told Jacqueline Leiner in an interview.[9] And in the re-creation the images are all-important as well as consistent from one poem to another. He has always written one and the same poem, according to what he told Jeannine Cahen in another interview.[10] The images – because they are recurrent – validate this claim. Césaire's poetic objectives, which can be called orphic, also contribute to this coherence. Like the surrealists Césaire supposes the poet to have special insight, or prescience, drawn from what Gregson Davis calls the "vatic unconscious" (*NVC*, 17), an insight that makes possible the prediction of the future and the conjuration of the present (Martinique) and the past (Africa). Césaire, by his own admission, seeks to break through, to descend into the depths to find "the fundamental negro." In this we discern the orphic nature of his poetic quest.

While taking different points of view, while adopting various personas, while enlisting many kinds of metaphor and many kinds of discourse, Césaire is constantly preoccupied with the problems of colonialization, of decolonialization, and of the revolution that will either succeed or fail in its effort to overcome racism and oppression. Add to that his obsession with fixing the poem, with the desire to bring back a poem of epic and tragic sweep and the potential failures inherent in that quest, and we readily recognize Césaire as a major author of the twentieth century, one whose works present a coherence and a single-mindedness within their broad vision.

Conclusion

In the preceding pages we have seen how Césaire's work, be it prose, poetry, or drama, expresses the need for revolution, for change in a flawed and prejudiced world. One of Césaire's chief strategies has been to mount a portrait of the ideal black man, the "culture hero" often of historical significance, often forgotten and in need of revival – a revered man who is made a scapegoat or model for his race, for humankind. It was not until Césaire presented Toussaint Louverture in *Cahier d'un retour* and in his later nonfiction study that his importance was recognized. And yet Césaire's efforts not only raised Toussaint to an iconic level, but they also succeeded in pointing to a new way of telling the story to any would-be historiographers.

Césaire's selection of historical figures is more than a simple search for role models (Toussaint, for example) or a hook for a cautionary tale (Christophe, for example). These individuals function also as irreversible proof that the black man is not just now beginning to "create a history" but has undergone a past that is a part of the record. Like the word *dog* or the word *disaster* (the latter of which Jean-Claude Bajeux [192] shows to be a *"mot-clé"* [key word], synthesizing the collective abuses blacks have suffered), the name "Toussaint Louverture" or just "Toussaint" comes, as a result of the poet-prophet's message, to be a *mot-clé* or, even better, a *mot-image*.[1] Indeed, it manages to signal the embodiment of revolt, revolution, leadership, passion (suffering), and the sum total of all that negritude represents, including its cultural load and commitment. To some extent, and despite a certain charge of rigidity associated with it, the same can be said of Lumumba's name, while, on the other hand, the very name "King Christophe" can evoke the flawed enterprise, the monumental failure that often brings with it earthly immortality, though not sainthood. In Césaire's case the emphasis is on the undertaking for itself.

Consequently, the historiographer Césaire vies with the poet Cé

saire in the telling of the particular story, and the history that is the
focus of the "chronicle plays" *(Christophe* and *Une saison au
Congo)* is elucidated by the "morality plays" *(Et les chiens se taisaient* and *Une tempête).* Likewise, the deafness and the aphasia that
result from centuries of brutal treatment vie with the voice and the
telling, and, more importantly, with the writing of the story and its
meaning (e.g., "ci-gît" in *Ferrements),* these being the tasks of the
poet-prophet-historiographer.

It is not surprising that in the poetry the message conveyed
erupts like the volcano of Mont-Pelé, whereas in the essays it is conveyed with less imagery but just as much emotion and force. Césaire's triple function as visionary poet, prophet, and historiographer
is a constant of his work. This triumvirate of roles, all calling for
commitment and action, is in fact more valid and meaningful than
the genre-dividing by which Césaire is incessantly called a poet who
has turned dramatist in order to carry his "message" more readily to
the people – who supposedly understand plays better than poems,
and, according to Sembène Ousmane, films even better – and who
then has turned from plays to essays, by which he presumably dis-
courses with black intellectuals or, for that matter, with any intellectuals.

However we may categorize him, we must agree that Césaire is
the negritude poet he defines, for as Janheiz Jahn understands him,
the negritude poet will be a word magician (the skillful manipulator
of Muntu and Nommo), messenger, spokesman, sponsor, and inter-
preter of Africa for the outside world. He will educate from within
and create visions of what ought to be. In rhythm, which is at the
very foundation of negritude poetry, Césaire "rediscovers himself in
the Universe" (Jahn 1968b, 249).

This complex relationship of the poet to his poem – and more
largely to the future of cosmic creativity – is not without its simultaneous debts to Leo Frobenius's Païdeuma, to the Bergson/Teilhard
de Chardin tradition, and to African ideas of poetry and cosmology.
The least one can say is that Césaire is a Caribbean poet; the most is
that Césaire in his poetry reflects not only a polycultural vision but
also a polypolar and an intergalactic one. Moreover, although Césaire is in many ways allied to the surrealist movement – and certainly
Breton thought so – he greatly differs from continental poets in that,
like all African poets, he sees dominion over the word as an essential

obligation of the poet, whereas the European surrealist renounces his command of words and opts instead for automatic writing. Besides, even in his war on reason Césaire is less allied to the continental surrealists than might at first seem apparent, since his war is specifically on the pseudo-reason of the Europeans.

The principal modes Césaire adopted to convey his poetic and political messages are nonetheless surrealist, dramatic, lyrical, and epic; the tone is sometimes threnodic, sometimes grandiose, and often ironic. Despite some comic scenes, Césaire's work on the whole seems humorless. Some critics – notably Eshleman following Arnold, but also Jacqueline Leiner[2] – see in his work a humor, and often a black humor, with debts to Lautréamont, the surrealists, Freud, and others (an often-cited example is his retort to the European rationalists that "2 + 2 = 5"). This seems less an instance of humor than of Césaire's insistence on offering alternative, viable systems reliant on the emotions and a quasi-mystical vision. Irony, not humor, is a powerful hallmark of Césaire's writing, and one of the problems in this discussion revolves around the fact that some critics tend to equate humor or black humor with irony and sarcasm, whereas by strictest definitions irony enters into black humor, perhaps, but is not its equivalent.

When considering Césaire's humor, one should above all take into account his ability at burlesque and parody, seen most conspicuously in *Christophe* and *Une saison au Congo*. To the extent that satire may be comic, this, along with his irony, is Césaire's most successful comic bid. Still, the passages where pain, suffering, and bitterness are in the ascendancy are far more trenchant and far more memorable than any touches of humor we may find along the way.

Some critics would not include Césaire in a panorama of African literature:[3] they would say he is, strictly speaking, a Caribbean poet. Others would put him in such a panorama, as an example of a poet of the "African continuum." Still others would put him in a survey of contemporary French poetry from the Continent without further ado. Césaire does not insist on a nationality: he is "open to all the winds of the world" (*Cahier*, 119) but at the same time is the defendent of his race. Lilyan Kesteloot best describes the situation when she writes, "[Césaire] is, along with a few other rare poets (Walt Whitman, Cendrars, Neruda, Maïakowski), a member of that race of poets who are plugged into the planet, into the cosmos. That is why Césaire has never admitted that his mind, or his three souls [Caribbean, African, European] have any boundary, or that knowledge has any limit, or inspiration any bonds, poetry being for him and by its essence, the miraculous space where his total liberty is realized" (*AC*, 295).[4] There is very possibly no better way to epitomize his position and his accomplishment.

Notes and References

Introduction

1. Frantz Fanon, *Black Skin, White Masks* (1952; New York: Grove Press, 1967), 23; hereafter cited in the text.

2. Jack Corzani, *La Littérature des Antilles-Guyane françaises*, vol. 1 (Fort-de-France, Martinique: Editions Désormeaux, 1978), 194-96; hereafter cited in the text.

3. Gérard Georges Pigeon, "Interview avec Aimé Césaire à Fort-de-France, le 12 janvier, 1977," *Cahiers césairiens* 3 (Spring 1977): 1-6; hereafter cited in the text.

4. Jean Wagner, *Black Poets of the United States* (Urbana: University of Illinois Press, 1973), 230-31; hereafter cited in the text.

5. Susan Frutkin, *Aimé Césaire: Black between Worlds* (Washington, D.C.: Center for Advanced International Studies, 1973), 27; hereafter cited in the text.

6. Beverley Ormerod, *An Introduction to the French Caribbean Novel* (London: Heinemann, 1985), 30; hereafter cited in the text.

7. Keith O. Tribble, "La Réception des oeuvres des fondateurs de la négritude en URSS," *Oeuvres et critiques* 3, no. 2, and 4, no. 1 (Fall 1979): 65; hereafter cited in the text.

8. Mbawil a Mpaang Ngal, *Aimé Césaire: Un homme à la recherche d'une patrie* (1975; Dakar, Abidjan: Nouvelles Editions Africaines, 1983); hereafter cited in the text.

9. Leo Frobenius, an antirationalist ethnologist whom Senghor considered a forerunner of negritude concepts by his insistence on a "vision of the whole, or ensemble" when considering societies, especially those of Africa, was "discovered" by Césaire, who then lent his book to Léopold Senghor. Among the most important readings on Césaire and Frobenius are those by Senghor in the journal *Ethiopiques* and Suzanne Césaire in the journal *Tropiques*.

10. The far-right writings of Arthur de Gobineau (1816-82), including *Essay on the Inequality of the Human Races* (1853-55), not only defended the racist views of his time, such as Aryan superiority, but also shared with Marx the concept of directing loyalty to class and race, although unity through miscegenation and the tendency of urbanization and industriali-

zation to destroy classes and states were for Marx an ideal and for Gobineau a disaster. "Gobinism," essentially pessimistic because its author sees no solution to racial problems, has been plumbed by twentieth-century racists, and while it became one of the underpinnings of the Holocaust it obviously still has followers in one form or another. See *Gobineau: Selected Political Writings*, ed. Michael D. Biddiss (New York: Harper & Row, 1970), 71; hereafter referred to in the text as "Biddiss."

11. Corzani, *La Littérature des Antilles-Guyane françaises;* Graziano Benelli, "L'Oeuvre de Césaire en Italie," *Cahiers césairiens* (Spring 1974): 9-19; Tribble, "La Réception des oeuvres des fondateurs de la négritude en URSS"; Roger Dorsinville, "Réception de la littérature antillaise au Sénégal," *Oeuvres et critiques* 3, no. 2 (Fall 1979): 21ff.; and Max Dorsinville, "Césaire au Québec," *Oeuvres et critiques* 4, no. 1 (Fall 1979): 229ff. These works are hereafter cited in the text.

12. The point is widely argued and has been the subject of much of Chinua Achebe's critical writing. In the case of Césaire, one excellent paper on the subject was delivered by Jean-Marie Salien at the Modern Language Association Convention in December 1981, "Négritude et lutte des classes dans *La Tragédie du roi Christophe* d'Aimé Césaire: Essai de sociocritique."

Chapter One

1. Jacques Chevrier, *Littérature nègre* (Paris: Armand Colin, 1974); hereafter cited in the text.

2. Césaire was not the first to write of Toussaint – Lamartine had written a play of some interest in the nineteenth century, as had others. There had even been an opera devoted to his story. But Césaire told it from a black perspective – a postrevolutionary, anticolonial, postcolonial perspective, one of outrage and indignation at the fact that after so much sacrifice so little had improved for the world's blacks.

3. Maryse Condé, *"Cahier d'un retour au pays natal": Profil d'une oeuvre* (Paris: Hatier, 1978), 8; hereafter cited in the text.

4. Thomas Hale, *Les Ecrits d'Aimé Césaire: Bibliographie commentée* (Montreal: Les Presses de l'Université de Montréal, 1978); hereafter cited in the text.

5. Ronnie Scharfman, *"Engagement" and the Language of the Subject in the Poetry of Aimé Césaire* (Gainesville: University Presses of Florida, 1987); hereafter cited in the text.

6. See Jahnheiz Jahn, "Nommo," a chapter in *Muntu* (New York: Grove Press, 1968); hereafter referred to in the text as "Jahn 1968a."

7. *Cahier d'un retour au pays natal/Notebook of a Return to My Native Land*, bilingual ed., trans. Emile Snyder (Paris: Présence Africaine, 1971), 18; hereafter referred to in the text as *Cahier*.

8. *Cahier d'un retour au pays natal*, trans. Jan[is] Pallister in *The Bruised Reed* (Sherbrooke, Canada: Editions Naaman, 1978), 66. The portions of *Cahier* translated therein (66-75) are hereafter referred to in the text as "Pallister 1978."

9. *Patyura* is a type of meadow or pastureland.

10. Portions of *Cahier d'un retour au pays natal* are translated in Marie Collins, *Black Poets in French* (New York: Charles Scribner's Sons, 1972), 215-17; hereafter referred to in the text as "Collins."

11. For a questionable discussion of the role of cannibalism in Césaire, see Clayton Eshleman in *Aimé Césaire: The Collected Poetry*, ed. Clayton Eshleman and Annette Smith (Berkeley: University of California Press, 1983), 13; hereafter referred to in the text as *CP*. One might add that in African societies the custom of cannibalism, like that of head-hunting, has to do with vanquishing one's enemies and taking their power.

12. Eric Sellin, *"Négritude:* Status or Dynamics?" *Esprit créateur* 10, no. 3 (Fall 1970): 173; hereafter cited in the text.

13. My translation of this passage (*The Bruised Reed*, 70) – a passage so important for its definition of negritude, and one quoted in the Mazrui series – may give a somewhat different feeling and contains lines Collins omits:

> . . . but those without whom the earth would not be the earth
> their humped posture increasingly benign as the
>   earth evermore abandons
> the earth
> and they a granary in which the earth's essence is
>   preserved and ripened
> my negritude is not a stone, its deafness flung
>   against the day's clamor
> my negritude is not a speck of dead moisture on
>   the dead eye of the earth
> my negritude is neither a tower nor a cathedral
>
> it plunges into the red flesh of the soil
> it plunges into the burning flesh of the sun
> it bores holes in the opaque affliction of its upright
>   patience.

14. With reference to voodoo, to the sorcerer, to the royal kailcedrate tree, to the African royalty of history (amazons of the king of Dahomey, princes of Ghana with 800 camels), to the continent as "gigantically caterpillaring as far as the Spanish foot of Europe," with reference also to Africa's "nakedness . . . where the scythe of Death swings wide" (*Cahier*, 67).

15. Emile Snyder, "A Reading of Aimé Césaire's *Return to My Native Land*," *Esprit créateur* 10, no. 3 (Fall 1970): 210; hereafter cited in the text.

16. In "Le Bateau ivre" Rimbaud exclaims, "May my keel erupt; may I put to sea." In "Mauvais Sang" he writes, "Science, the new nobility. Progress! The world is on the move! Why would it not turn . . . *De profundis, Domine*, how stupid I am . . . I am a stupid beast, a negro. But I can be saved. You are false negroes, you maniacs, ferocious, avaricious. . . . The whites land. The canon! One must submit to baptism, wear clothes, work." Before Césaire, Rimbaud in this passage sensed the duplicity of "scientific progress" and vicariously experienced the profound stigmata of racism. He also sensed the ironies of "Christianizing" the black races. (I have quoted from Rimbaud's *Oeuvres* [Paris: Mercure de France, 1949], 66, 199, 202, 203. My translations.)

17. André Ntonfo, *L'Homme et l'identité dans le roman des Antilles et Guyane françaises* (Sherbrooke, Canada: Editions Naaman, 1982), 12; hereafter cited in the text.

18. Michel Benamou, "Entretien avec Aimé Césaire à Fort-de-France, le 14 février, 1973," *Cahiers césairiens* 1 (Spring 1974): 4-8; hereafter cited in the text.

19. A. James Arnold, *Modernism and Negritude* (Cambridge, Mass.: Harvard University Press, 1981), 30; hereafter cited in the text.

20. Graziano Benelli, *Aimé Césaire* (Firenze, Italy: La Nuova Italia, 1975); hereafter cited in the text.

21. See Lilyan Kesteloot, "Alchimie d'un poème," and Daniel Racine, "Césaire et la problématique de la culture antillaise," both in *Aimé Césaire, ou l'athanor d'un alchimiste* (Paris: Editions Caribéennes, 1987), 295 and 329, respectively. Essays from this collection are hereafter referred to in the text as *AC*.

22. James Clifford, "A Politics of Neologism: Aimé Césaire," chapter 7 of *The Predicament of Culture* (Cambridge, Mass.: Harvard University Press, 1988), 176-77; hereafter cited in the text.

23. Condé (in *Profil d'une oeuvre*, 53) fleshes out these arguments, claiming that it is not surrealism that has been behind Césaire's audacities of language. The impulse, she says, is more profound than that, for he intends to forge a language that will give an account of his being both black and Antillais. (Her proofs are problematic and her comparisons with Nicolás Guillén not appropriate, as it has been established that Césaire did not know this poet until well after his poetic enterprise and procedures were firmly established.)

24. See Hugh Fox, ed., *First Fire: Central and South American Indian Poetry* (Garden City, N.Y.: Doubleday, 1978), 141.

25. Gregson Davis sees a relationship between Césaire's writing and Alejo Charpentier's concept of magic surrealism. The idea would be that

the American artist experiences the marvelous in his daily existence and therefore has no need to invent the domain of fantasy, as would be the case for the European surrealist. The European surrealist fabricates a world he has never really directly perceived, whereas, according to Davis, Césaire reflects a Martinique reality; the marvelous in his poetry originates in the real, or arises from an unexpected mutation of reality. See *Non-Vicious Circle: Twenty Poems of Aimé Césaire*, ed. and trans. Gregson Davis (Stanford, Calif.: Stanford University Press, 1984), 9-14; hereafter referred to in the text as *NVC*.

26. Gospel – that is, the Gospel or the Good News of Negritude, of a new era for the race.

27. I elaborate on my ideas about Sartre's essay in *The Bruised Reed*. "Orphée noir" has been the brunt of considerable criticism since its publication in Léopold Senghor's *Anthologie de la nouvelle poésie nègre et malgache* (Paris: Presses Universitaires Françaises, 1948). The essay has been found to proceed in its analysis of the collection's poems along the then-in-vogue existential and Hegelian lines. One of its major shortcomings, however, is that it fixes on race to the exclusion of class and therefore falls short of considering the works from the perspective of the Marxist ideal of a classless society. (In *Black Skin, White Masks* Fanon discusses Sartre's essay in acerbic tones.) While scholars might fault the content of this essay for a variety of reasons, all would concede that Sartre's name lent the anthology great credibility at a time when the poets represented therein had little or no fame.

28. Senghor, in his *Liberté I: Négritude et humanisme* (Paris: Seuil, 1964), advances his first of many explanations of the term and the philosophy behind it. Negritude is conceived of as a new humanism, just as feminism has been seen as a new humanism by continental French feminists, particularly "Choisir" president Gisèle Halimi, who writes, "One must be of bad faith, not to perceive the 'humanist' dimension of feminism" (*Elle*, 10 June 1978; cited in *Ensemble: Culture et société*, 2d ed., ed. Raymond F. Comeau et al. [New York: Holt, Rinehart & Winston, 1982], 28; my translation).

29. Graziano Benelli, "L'Ecriture des libertés," in *Aimé Césaire, ou l'athanor d'un alchimiste*, 28.

30. Roger Toumson, "Une expérience des limites," in *Aimé Césaire, ou l'athanor d'un alchimiste*, 120-22.

31. Lilyan Kesteloot and B[arthélemy] Kotchy, *Aimé Césaire, l'homme et l'oeuvre* (Paris: Présence Africaine, 1973), 235; hereafter cited in the text.

32. Maximilien Laroche, "Lecture filmique du *Cahier d'un retour au pays natal*," in *Aimé Césaire, ou l'athanor d'un alchimiste*, 165-69.

33. See G. D. Killam, *African Writers on African Writing* (Evanston, Ill.: Northwestern University Press, 1973), 152-53, and John Erickson, *African Fiction in French* (York, S.C.: French Literature Publications, 1979), 188-89.

Chapter Two

1. Bertrand Visage, in Beaumarchais's *Dictionnaire des litteratures de langue française* (Paris: Bordas, 1984), 400-401. It is hard to understand why Visage speaks of a mixture of prose and poetry; more accurately, we have "prose poems" throughout. Césaire's surrealism is beautifully epitomized in Jean-Claude Michel's *Les Ecrivains noirs et le surréalisme* (Sherbrooke, Canada: Editions Naaman, 1982), especially chapter 4, where he studies Césaire's poetic language, surrealist *art poétique,* verbal automatism, poetic image, and individuality and originality. He concludes with comments on negritude.

Senghor has clarified the role of images in negritude poetry in at least two important essays, "Comme les lamantins vont boire à la source" (in *Poèmes* [Paris: Seuil, 1973]) and "Dialogue sur la poésie francophone" (in *Elegies majeures* [Paris: Seuil, 1979]). In these pieces Senghor explains that the analogical image of Francophone negritude poetry has no function until it becomes rhythm. He also traces the history of poetry as vision and shows that, since the Renaissance, French poetry has not been characterized by vision; rather, poetry as vision comes from the Greek or Mediterranean tradition and is therefore linked to Africa. While Western discourse, which is enlisted for French poetry, is premeditated, African poetry arises from inspiration. Additionally, what counts for today's Francophone poets is the *object* of the poem, and this object is an ontological vision of the universe, of man in the universe. Senghor's concept of image, of poetry as vision, and the notion of object in that vision is quite applicable to Césaire's work, even though the latter is not, strictly speaking, African.

2. On the vast array of images, see Keith Louis Walker, *La Cohésion poétique de l'oeuvre césairienne* (Paris: Editions Jean-Michel Place, 1979); hereafter cited in the text.

3. John Erickson, "Le Discours révolutionnaire dans *Les Armes miraculeuses,"* in *Aimé Césaire, ou l'athanor d'un alchimiste,* 53-62; hereafter cited in the text.

4. Aliko Songolo, *Aimé Césaire, une poétique de la découverte* (Paris: L'Harmattan, 1985), 108; hereafter cited in the text.

5. Bernadette Cailler, *Proposition poétique: Une lecture de l'oeuvre d'Aimé Césaire* (Sherbrooke, Canada: Editions Naaman, 1976), 73; hereafter cited in the text.

6. Eloise Brière, "Poésie québécoise et situation coloniale," *Revue francophone de Louisiane* 2, no. 1 (Spring 1988): 9-18.

7. *Les Armes miraculeuses* (Paris: Gallimard, 1970), 52; hereafter referred to in the text as *AM.* The translation here is my own.

8. Eric Sellin, *"Soleil cou coupé," Romance Notes* 14, no. 1 (Autumn 1972): 13-16; hereafter cited in the text.

9. *Corps perdu,* in *Cadastre* (Paris: Seuil, 1961), 83.

10. *Ferrements* (Paris: Seuil, 1960), 32; hereafter referred to in the text as *F*.

11. Breton's interest in revolution, and even in failed revolutionary heroes like Henri Christophe and Patrice Lumumba, is studied by Anna Balakian in "André Breton's *Les Etats généraux:* Revolution and Poetry," *French Review* 62, no. 6 (May 1989): 1008-16.

12. Bernadette Cailler, "'Crevasse,' métaphore vive du texte," in *Aimé Césaire ou l'athanor d'un alchimiste*, 97-102; hereafter cited as in the text.

13. Antoine Bolamba, *Esanzo*, trans. Jan[is] Pallister (Sherbrooke, Canada: Editions Naaman, 1977), 42. All the great themes of negritude are found in this collection, as Senghor states in his Introduction. Expressed in "metalanguage" (the language of the sacred), these poems by the Congolese Bolamba, like those of Césaire, express humanism, poetic and political revolt, and revolt against rationalism.

Chapter Three

1. In this chapter I focus primarily on the 1944 poetic version of *Et les chiens se taisaient* (I address variants where appropriate). See Ernstpeter Ruhe's intricate analysis of the poem and the theatrical adaptation ("Aimé Césaire et Janheinz Jahn," in *Aimé Césaire, ou l'athanor d'un alchimiste*, 201-21), which contains important contrasting passages in its appendices.

2. Claude McKay, *Selected Poems*, ed. John Dewey (New York: Bookman, 1953), 36.

3. *Et les chiens se taisaient – Tragédie (arrangement théâtral)* (Paris: Présence Africaine, 1956), 43. This theatrical version is hereafter referred to in the text by page number alone.

4. Lilyan Kesteloot, *Anthologie négro-africaine* (Verviers, Belgium: Marabout Université, 1967), 96.

5. For a study of the Christ figure in African-American and African poetry, see Charlotte Bruner, "The Image of the Christ Black," *College Language Association Journal* 24, no. 3 (March 1981): 352-68. Here, however, Césaire is not a prominent target.

6. Note that in the poem "Ibis-Anubis" from *Noria* Césaire speaks of the Word (the poetic Word) as a great horned owl (*grand duc*) that hovers over him muzzled like Anubis (*CP*, 388-89).

7. Toni Morrison, *Song of Solomon* (New York: Signet, 1978), 52.

8. See Russell G. Hamilton, *Voices from an Empire* (Minneapolis: University of Minnesota Press, 1975), 213-14.

9. Albert Owusu-Sarpong, *Le Temps historique dans l'oeuvre théâtrale d'Aimé Césaire* (Sherbrooke, Canada: Editions Naaman, 1986); hereafter cited in the text.

10. Rodney Harris, *L'Humanisme dans le théâtre d'Aimé Césaire* (Sherbrooke, Canada: Editions Naaman, 1973).

11. Janis L. Pallister, "Historical Figures as *Exempla* in the Work of Aimé Césaire," *French Literature Series* 7 (1981): 124-29.

12. Francis Anani Joppa, *L'Engagement des écrivains africains noirs de langue française* (Sherbrooke, Canada: Editions Naaman, 1982), 237; hereafter cited in the text. Fanon maintains that the African revolution can only be brought about through violence.

Chapter Four

1. As noted in my discussion of *Cahier d'un retour au pays natal*, *lambi* is the conch shell used to send messages among the Haitian revolutionaries – that is, to call the slaves to rebellion against the master. Jacques Cousteau's 1986 video "Haiti, Waters of Sorrow" shows the Haitians sending messages on the *lambi*. The video also depicts the *pirogues*.

2. See Henock Trouillet, *Le Gouvernement du roi Henri Christophe* (Port-au-Prince: Imprimerie Centrale, 1974).

3. *The Tragedy of King Christophe*, trans. Ralph Manheim (New York: Grove Press, 1979), 7-8; hereafter referred to in the text by page number alone.

4. Born in Guinea in 1758, Dessalines was a mulatto and among the first of Haiti's revolutionaries. Having become general of Toussaint's brigade, he helped to drive the English from the island and in 1803 revolted against General Rochambeau (Jean Baptiste de Vimeur, comte de Rochambeau) and proclaimed independence for Saint-Domingue. Named Emperor Jacques I in 1804, he was perceived as a tyrant and was assassinated at Jacmel in 1806 during a coup against him. Dessalines is the object of the Félix Morisseau-Leroy poem "Méci, papa Dessalines." One can see in him a type of Papa Doc.

5. Jean-Claude Bajeux has discussed the colonized black man's frequent and pathetic effort to imitate the white, with special reference to Luis Palés Matos (*Antilia retrouvée: Etude comparée de trois poètes noirs antillais* [Paris: Editions Caribéennes, 1983], 153-56).

6. Interestingly enough, this scene was not part of the original version of the play, as published in several numbers of the journal *Présence africaine* in 1962. I follow this French version here; Présence Africaine published the play in book form in 1963.

7. David L. Dunn, "Interview with Aimé Césaire on a New Approach to *La Tragédie du roi Christophe* and *Une saison au Congo*," *Cahiers césairiens* 4 (Fall 1980): 3; hereafter cited in the text.

8. Janheiz Jahn, *Neo-African Literature* (New York: Grove Press, 1968), 122, 135, 136; hereafter referred to in the text as "Jahn 1968b."

9. Frederick Ivor Case, "Sango Oba Ko So: Le Vodoun dans *La Tragédie du roi Christophe*," *Cahiers césairiens* 2 (Fall 1975): 15; hereafter cited in the text.

10. See *Présence africaine*, 11, no. 39 (1962): 194 for the exact text of this missing passage.

11. This proclamation did not appear in the original version of scene 1 (*Présence africaine* 16, no. 44 [1962]: 108).

12. Rodney Harris informs us that the song of *la petite noire* or romance of Ourika does exist ("The Scrupulous Aimé Césaire," *Cahiers césairiens* 2 [Fall 1975]: 27). The second version presented by Césaire is the "correct" one; it is a nineteenth-century piece by Ulrich Güttinger.

13. Langston Hughes, *The Langston Hughes Reader* (1958; New York: George Braziller, 1965), 88.

14. See James Ferguson, *Papa Doc, Baby Doc: Haiti and the Duvaliers* (London: Basil Blackwell, 1989).

15. René Ménil, "Le Romanesque et le réalisme dans *La Tragédie du roi Christophe*," *Action*, January 1965; hereafter cited in the text. Hervé Fuyet et al., "Décolonisation et classes sociales dans *La Tragédie du roi Christophe*," *French Review* 46, no. 6 (May 1973): 1101-6; hereafter cited in the text.

16. Lilian Pestre de Almeida, "Rire haitien, rire africain: Le Comique dans *La Tragédie du roi Christophe* de Césaire," *Présence francophone* 10 (Spring 1975): 59-71.

17. Maximilien Laroche, "*La Tragédie du roi Christophe*," *Etudes littéraires* 6, no. 1 (April 1973): 495; hereafter cited in the text.

18. Janis L. Pallister, "Time, Tense, and Tempo in the Work of Jean Dieudonné Garçon," *Esprit créateur* 42, no. 2 (Summer 1977): 159-67.

19. Quoted in Bakary Traoré, "Le Théâtre africain: réalités et perspectives," in *Actes du colloque d'Abidjan* (Paris: Présence Africaine, 1971), 59.

20. "Culture et colonisation" (speech before the First International Congress of Black Writers, Paris), special issue of *Présence africaine*, September 1956; hereafter referred to in the text as "Culture."

Chapter Five

1. Bernard Zadi-Zaourou, *Césaire entre deux cultures* (Dakar: Nouvelles Editions Africains, 1978); hereafter cited in the text.

2. See "Hommage to Frantz Fanon," *Présence africaine* (1962): 131-34.

3. For an exposé of the role of these nationalities in the fight for the Congo, see Frantz Fanon, *Toward the African Revolution* (New York: Grove Press, 1967), 196.

4. Marcel Odden, "Les Tragédies de la décolonisation," in *Le Théâtre moderne depuis la deuxième guerre mondiale* (Paris: CNRS, 1967), 97.

5. Frederick Ivor Case, "Aimé Césaire et l'Occident chrétien," *Esprit créateur* 10, no. 3 (Fall 1970): 256.

6. Jonathan Ngaté, *"Mauvais sang* de Rimbaud et *Cahier d'un retour au pays natal* de Césaire: La Poésie au service de la révolution," *Cahiers césairiens* 3 (Spring 1977): 25-32.

7. Rodney Harris, "The English Translations of Césaire's Theater," *Cahiers césairiens* 1 (Spring 1974): 32-34.

8. Frédérique Dutoit, "Quand le Congo ne sera qu'une saison que le sang assaisonne," *Présence africaine* 64 (1967): 138-45.

9. Frantz Fanon, *Les Damnés de la terre* (Paris: Maspéro, 1961), 144.

10. *A Season in the Congo,* trans. Ralph Manheim (New York: Grove, 1969), 1; hereafter referred to in the text by page number alone. I occasionally refer to the French edition (Paris: Seuil, 1973).

11. David Lee Dunn, "Theatrical Metaphor, Alienation, and Nihilism in Two Plays by Aimé Césaire and Two Plays by Bertolt Brecht," Ph.D. diss. (Nashville: Vanderbilt University, 1975), 63. See also Dunn's interview with Césaire.

12. Clément Mbom, "La Femme dans le théâtre d'A.C.," in *Aimé Césaire, ou l'athanor d'un alchimiste,* 223-37; hereafter cited in the text. Mbom also has to his credit a book on Césaire's theater, *Le Théâtre d'Aimé Césaire, ou la primauté de l'universalité humaine* (Paris: Nathan, 1980).

13. Note the reference to his enemies as "dogs," a metaphor I have examined in chapter 3 and elsewhere.

14. Lilian de Pestre de Almeida, "Le Bestiaire symbolique dans *Une saison au Congo," Présence francophone* 13 (Fall 1976): 93-105.

Chapter Six

1. *Caliban,* in vol. 3 of Ernest Renan's *Oeuvres complètes,* ed. Henriette Psichari (Paris: Calmann-Lévy, 1949), 425.

2. *L'Eau de Jouvence,* also in vol. 3 of Renan's *Oeuvres complètes,* 440.

3. Lemuel Johnson, *High Life for Caliban* (Ann Arbor, Mich.: Ardis Publishers, 1973), 17; hereafter cited in the text.

4. Christophe Dailly, review of Rodney Harris's *L'Humanisme dans le théâtre d'Aimé Césaire, Oeuvres et critiques* 4, no. 1 (Fall 1979): 245-53; hereafter cited in the text.

5. *Une tempête* (Paris: Seuil, 1969), 13; hereafter referred to in the text by page number alone. My translations.

Chapter Seven

1. *Discours sur le colonialisme* (Paris: Présence Africaine, 1955, 1970), 9; hereafter referred to in the text as *Discours*. My translations.

2. Lautréamont's Maldoror and Baudelaire's *chiffonnier*. The symbolic hero of Lautréamont's 1868 fantastic epic *Les Chants de Maldoror* suffers all humanity's indignities. It is not surprising that Césaire seeks to vindicate Maldoror, a nineteenth-century *révolté*, who rebels against God and is subsequently changed into a minotaur. Lautréamont's work is considered a precursor of surrealism, and we should not be surprised that Césaire wrote an essay entitled "Isidore Ducasse comte de Lautréamont" for *Tropiques* (no. 7, February) in 1943. Of equal interest is the reference to Baudelaire's poem "Le Vin des chiffonniers," which describes the misery of the *chiffonnier* and his recourse to wine to relieve his suffering and insignificance. Césaire alludes indirectly to the poor and downtrodden taking to alcohol, with the colonizers taking advantage of such widespread incapacity to dominate the people further. The poem is found in *Les Fleurs du mal* but should be considered intertextually with the prose poem "Du Vin et du haschisch" of *Paradis artificiels*. Baudelaire, too, is a type of the *révolté*.

3. Hubert Juin, *Aimé Césaire, poète noir* (Paris: Présence Africaine, 1956), 81; hereafter cited in the text.

4. See Priska Degras's "Stratégie et leçon du *Discours sur le colonialisme*: L'Organization de la parole pour l'autre," in *Aimé Césaire, ou l'athanor d'un alchimiste*, 171ff., for further analysis of this essay.

5. Preface to Daniel Guérin's *Antilles décolonisées* (Paris: Présence Africaine, 1956), 12-14. Here Césaire recognized that de facto inequality still existed after departmentalization.

6. *Lettre à Maurice Thorez* (Paris: Présence Africaine, 1956).

7. Colin Legum, *Pan-Africanism: A Short Political Guide* (New York: Praeger, 1965).

8. Published again as *Toussaint Louverture: La Révolution française et le problème colonial*, with a preface by Charles-André Julien (Paris: Présence Africaine, 1961). (This essay was first published in 1960 in the "Portraits de l'histoire" series by the Club Français du Livre, Paris.) I follow the version provided in *Aimé Césaire*, ed. M. and S. Battestini (Paris: Fernand Nathan, 1967); hereafter referred to in the text as *Toussaint*. My translations.

9. Jacqueline Leiner, "Entretien," in the Césaire edition of *Tropiques*, vol. 1 (Paris: Jean-Michel Place, 1978), xiv-xv.

10. Jeannine Cahen, "Interview with Aimé Césaire," *Afrique action* 21 (November 1960).

Conclusion

1. *Mot-image.* By this I mean a word that in and of itself brings up an image. It is a term often applied to classical literature, particularly in analyzing Corneillean drama, but it seems quite appropriate to use it here as well.

2. Jacqueline Leiner, "Césaire et les problèmes du langage chez un écrivian francophone," *Esprit créateur* 17, no. 2 (Summer 1977): 140-41.

3. For instance, Jacques Nantet, *Panorama de la littérature noire d'expression française* (Paris: Fayard, 1972).

4. This is my translation; the original passage has "Walt Withman."

Selected Bibliography

PRIMARY WORKS (FRENCH)

Collected Works

Aimé Césaire. Edited by M. and S. Battestini. Paris: Fernand Nathan, 1967.

Oeuvres complètes. 3 volumes. Edited by Jean-Paul Césaire. Fort-de-France, Martinique: Editions Désormeaux, 1976. Includes the 17 *Noria* poems.

Poetry

Les Armes miraculeuses. 1944. Paris: Gallimard, 1970. Contains *Et les chiens se taisaient* as poem.

Cadastre. Paris: Seuil, 1961. Consists of *Soleil cou coupé* (1948) and *Corps perdu* (1949).

Cahier d'un retour au pays natal. 1939, 1944 (preface by André Breton). Paris: Présence Africaine, 1971.

"Configurations." In *Aimé Césaire, ou l'anthanor d'un alchimiste.* Paris: Editions Caribéennes, 1987. Collection of papers presented at the 1985 international colloquy on his work.

Ferrements. Paris: Seuil, 1960.

Moi, laminaire. Paris: Seuil, 1982.

Soleil cou coupé. 1948. Nendeln: Kraus-Thomson Organization, Ltd., 1970.

Plays

Et les chiens se taisaient – Tragédie (Arrangement théâtral). Paris: Présence Africaine, 1956.

La Tragédie du roi Christophe. 1963. Paris: Présence Africaine, 1970.

La Tragédie du roi Christophe. In *Présence africaine* 11, no. 39 (1962): 168-98 [English ed., act 1]; 16, no. 44 (1962): 106-28 [English ed., act 2]; 18, no. 46 (1963): 114-34 [English ed., act 3].

Une saison au Congo. 1965. Paris: Seuil, 1973.

Une tempête. Paris: Seuil, 1969.

Nonfiction

"Culture et colonisation." *Présence africaine*, September 1956, 190-205. Paper presented at the First International Congress of Black Writers, Paris, 1956.

"Décolonisation pour les Antilles." *Présence africaine*, April-May 1956, 7-12.

"Deuil aux Antilles." *Présence africaine* (Third Trimester 1962): 221-22.

"Discours sur l'art africain." *Etudes littéraires* 6, no. 1 (April 1973): 99-109.

Discours sur le colonialisme. 1950. Paris: Présence Africaine, 1970.

"Esthéthique césairienne." *Etudes littéraires* 6, no. 1 (April 1973): 111-12.

"L'Homme de culture et ses responsabilités." *Présence africaine* 1 (March-April 1959): 116-22. Paper presented at the Second International Congress of Black Writers, Rome, 1959.

Lettre à Maurice Thorez. Paris: Présence Africaine, 1956.

Preface to *Antilles décolonisées*, by Daniel Guérin. Paris: Présence Africaine, 1956.

"Société et littérature dans les Antilles." *Etudes littéraires* 6, no. 1 (April 1973): 9-20.

Toussaint Louverture: La Révolution française et le problème colonial. Paris: Présence Africaine, 1961.

Tropiques. Edited by Aimé Césaire. 2 vols. Paris: Jean-Michel Place, 1978. Contains the essay "Poésie et connaissance," first given as a speech in Haiti on 28 September 1944, and an interview with Jacqueline Leiner.

PRIMARY WORKS (ENGLISH TRANSLATIONS)

Poetry

Aimé Césaire: The Collected Poetry. Edited and translated by Clayton Eshleman and Annette Smith. Berkeley: University of California Press, 1983.

Cadastre. 1961. Translated by Emile Snyder and Sanford Upson. New York: Third World Press, 1973.

Lost Body. Translated by Clayton Eshleman and Annette Smith; illustrated by Pablo Picasso. New York: Braziller, 1986.

Lyric and Dramatic Poetry. Translated by Clayton Eshleman and Annette Smith (Charlottesville: University of Virginia Press, 1990). Contains translations of *Moi, laminaire* and *Et les chiens se taisaient* and other poems.

Non-Vicious Circle: Twenty Poems of Aimé Césaire. Translated with introduction and commentary by Gregson Davis. Stanford, Calif.: Stanford University Press, 1984.

Notebook of a Return to My Native Land. Bilingual edition; translated by Emile Snyder. Paris: Présence Africaine, 1971. (A reworking of the translation by Lionel Abel and Yvan Goll [Brentano's, 1947].) Portions translated in *The Bruised Reed,* by Jan[is] Pallister (Sherbrooke, Canada: Editions Naaman, 1978), and *Black Poets in French,* by Marie Collins (New York: Charles Scribner's Sons, 1972).

Return to My Native Land. Translated by John Berger and Anna Bostock. Baltimore: Penguin, 1969.

Plays

A Season in the Congo. Translated by Ralph Manheim. New York: Grove Press, 1969.

A Tempest. Translated by Emile Snyder and Sanford Upson. New York: Third World Press, 1975.

Tragedy of King Christophe. Translated by Ralph Manheim. New York: Grove Press, 1970.

Nonfiction

"Crisis in the Overseas Departments; or, Crisis of the Departmental System." *Présence africaine* [English ed.] 8, no. 36 (1961): 100-102.

Discourse on Colonialism. Translated by by Joan Pinkham. New York: Monthly Review Press, 1972.

"Greetings to the New World." *Confrontations* 1, no 1 (Summer 1970).

"Hommage to Frantz Fanon." *Présence africaine* [English ed.] 12, no. 40 (1962): 131-34.

"Hommage to Jean Amrouche." *Présence africaine* [English ed.] 18, no. 46 (1963): 176-79.

"The Political Thought of Sékou Touré." *Présence africaine* [English ed.], n.s., 1, no. 29 (1960): 63-72.

Preface to *The West Indies and Their Future,* by Daniel Guérin. Translated by Austryn Wainhouse. London: Dobson Books, 1961.

SECONDARY WORKS

Aimé Césaire, ou l'athanor d'un alchimiste. Paris: Editions Caribéennes, 1987. Contains various papers on Césaire's work presented at a 1985 colloquy in Paris, many of which are cited in my text and in the notes (Kesteloot, Racine, Benelli, Toumson, Cailler, Erikson, Mbom, Ruhe).

Arnold, A. James. *Modernism and Negritude.* Cambridge, Mass.: Harvard University Press, 1981. A close analysis of Césaire's poetry collections as specimens of modernism.

Bajeux, Jean-Claude. *Antilia retrouvée.* Paris: Editions Caribéennes, 1983. Césaire as a Caribbean poet.

Balakian, Anna. "André Breton's *Les Etats généraux:* Revolution and Poetry." *French Review* 62, no. 6 (May 1989): 1008-16. A view of Breton's
attitude toward revolution; article faulted by complete lack of appara-
tus.

Benamou, Michel. "Entretien avec Aimé Césaire à Fort-de-France, le 14
février, 1973." *Cahiers césairiens* 1 (Spring 1974): 4-8. Conversation
with Césaire about his work.

_____. "Sémiotique du *Cahier d'un retour au pays natal.*" *Cahiers cé-
sairiens* 2 (1975): 3-8. A short semiotic analysis of Césaire's first long
poem, according to divisions made by a group presenting a reading of
the poem in Fort-de-France and other localities in Martinique.

Benelli, Graziano. *Aimé Césaire.* Firenze, Italy: La Nuova Italia, 1975. A
Marxist analysis of Césaire's work.

_____. "Césaire rilegge Shakespeare." *Annali* [Feltre, Italy] (1974): 321-28.
Influences of Shakespeare on Césaire.

_____. "L'Oeuvre de Césaire en Italie." *Cahiers césairiens* 1 (Spring 1974):
9-19. Reception of Césaire's work in Italy.

Biddiss, Michael D. *Gobineau: Selected Political Writings.* New York:
Harper & Row, 1970. Contains Gobineau's *Essay on the Inequality of
the Human Races* (1853-55), which has fed the currents of European
rightest racism for a century and a half, and which was studied and
criticized by negritude intellectuals, including Césaire.

Bolamba, Antoine. *Esanzo,* translated by Jan[is] Pallister. Sherbrooke,
Canada: Editions Naaman 1977. Edition and translation of the Congolese Bolamba's poetry, which displays a generally gentle and interi-
orized negritude orientation.

Brière, Eloise A. "Poésie québécoise et situation coloniale." *Revue francophone de Louisiane* 2, no. 1 (Spring 1988): 9-18. A look at Quebec poetry from the perspective of colonialism.

Bruner, Charlotte. "The Image of the Christ Black." *College Language Association Journal* 24, no. 3 (March 1981), 352-68. An analysis of various portrayals of Christ as a black.

_____. "The Meaning of Caliban in Black Literature Today." *Comparative
Literature Studies* 13, no. 3 (September 1976): 240-53.

Cahen, Jeannine. "Interview with Aimé Césaire." *Afrique Action,* 21
November 1960.

Cailler, Bernadette. *Proposition poétique. Une lecture de l'oeuvre d'Aimé
Césaire.* Sherbrooke, Canada: Editions Naaman, 1976. An oft-quoted
study of Césaire's poetry.

Case, Frederick Ivor. "Aimé Césaire et l'Occident chrétien." *Esprit créateur*
10, no. 3 (Fall 1970): 242-56. Césaire's critique of the Christian West
and Western Christianity.

_____. "Sango Oba Ko So: Le Vodoun dans *La Tragédie du Roi Christophe.*" *Cahiers césairiens* 2 (Fall 1975): 9-24. How voodoo figures in *Christophe.*

Césaire, Suzanne. "Léo Frobenius et le problème des civilisations." *Tropiques* 1 (April 1941): 27-36. An article by Césaire's wife on Frobenius's view of civilizations.

Chevrier, Jacques. *Littérature nègre.* Paris: Armand Colin, 1974. A short description of black literature.

Christophe, Marc-A. "Totalitarianism and Authoritarianism in Aimé Césaire's *La Tragédie du roi Christophe.*" *CLA Journal* 22 (1978): 31-45.

Clifford, James. "A Politics of Neologism: Aimé Césaire" Chapter 7 of *The Predicament of Culture: Twentieth-Century Ethnography, Literature, and Art.* Cambridge, Mass.: Harvard University Press, 1988.

Condé, Maryse. *"Cahier d'un retour au pays natal." Profil d'une oeuvre.* Paris: Hatier, 1978. A short but precise and reliable analysis of the *Cahier.*

Cook, Mercer, and Stephen E. Henderson. *The Militant Black Writer in Africa and the United States.* Madison: University of Wisconsin Press, 1969. Scattered references to Césaire, with passages from the *Cahier* in the Brentano translation.

Cornevin, Robert. *La Littérature d'Afrique noire de langue française.* Paris: Presses Universitaires de France, 1976. A panoramic study of black African literature in French.

_____. *Le Théâtre en Afrique noire et à Madagascar.* Paris: Le Livre Africain, 1970. An analysis of theatrical works by black playwrights of Africa and Madagascar.

Corzani, Jack. *La littérature des Antilles-Guyane françaises.* 6 vols. Fort-de-France, Martinique: Editions Désormeaux, 1978. Reference to Césaire in this lengthy study of Caribbean French literature.

Dailly, Christophe. Review of Rodney Harris's *L'Humanisme dans le théâtre d'Aimé Césaire. Oeuvres et critiques* 4, no. 1 (Fall 1979): 245-53.

Daninos, Guy. *"Une tempête* de Césaire ou le prélude d'une nouvelle renaissance." *Licorne* 9 (1985): 153-60.

Depestre, René. "Itinéraire d'un langage: De l'Afrique à la Caraïbbe. Entretien avec Aimé Césaire." *Europe* 612 (1980): 19ff. An interview between the two eminent black poets.

Dorsinville, Max. *Caliban without Prospero: Essay on Quebec and Black Literature* (Erin, Ontario: Porcepic, 1974). Discussion of *Une tempête.*

_____. "Césaire au Québec." *Oeuvres et critiques* 4, no. 1 (Fall 1979): 230-31. Reception of Césaire's work in Quebec.

Dunn, David L. "Interview [1974] with Aimé Césaire on a New Approach to *La Tragédie du roi Christophe* and *Une saison au Congo.*" *Cahiers césairiens* 4 (Fall 1980): 1-10.

_____. "Theatrical Metaphor, Alienation and Nihilism in Two Plays by Aimé Césaire and Two Plays by Bertold Brecht." Ph.D. dissertation (Vanderbilt University, 1975). Abstracted in *Cahiers césairiens* 3 (Spring 1977): 55-56. Dunn finds that both playwrights present their characters as having split personalities, as seeking transcendence, and as separating from their fellows. Césaire's characters, however, represent negritude rebellion against colonialism and Europeanism, whereas Brechtian characters renounce capitalism in favor of Marxist communism.

Duplessis, Yves. *Surrealism,* translated by Paul Capon (from 1950 text). Westport, Conn.: Greenwood Press, 1978. One of the classic studies in surrealism and its relationship to Marxism.

Dutoit, Frédérique. "Quand le Congo ne sera qu'une saison que le sang assaisonne." *Présence africaine* 64 (1967): 138-45. Predictions of bloodshed in the Congo at the point of decolonization.

Erickson, John. *African Fiction in French.* York, S.C.: French Literature Publications, 1979.

Esprit créateur (Fall 1970). Special issue on the Antilles.

Etudes littéraires 6, no. 1 (April 1973). Special issue on Césaire containing an article and two *discours* by Césaire, along with articles by Lilyan Kesteloot, Maximilien Laroche, Thomas Hale, and other scholars.

Fanon, Frantz. *Black Skin, White Masks.* 1952. New York: Grove Press, 1967. Shows how blacks may be obliged to take on "masks." Césaire calls this the "essential book" about colonialism and the human consequences of colonization and racism.

_____. *A Dying Colonialism.* New York: Grove Press, 1965.

_____. *Toward the African Revolution.* 1964. New York: Grove Press, 1967. Important pages on Algeria's revolution against French dominion.

_____. *The Wretched of the Earth.* 1961. New York: Grove Press, 1967. Scrutinizes racism and colonialism. Césaire calls this the "essential book" about decolonization.

Ferguson, James. *Papa Doc, Baby Doc: Haiti and the Duvaliers.* London: Basil Blackwell, 1989. To be read for relationship to *Christophe.*

Filostrat, Christian. "La Négritude et la 'Conscience raciale et révolution sociale' d'Aimé Césaire." *Présence francophone* 21 (Fall 1980): 119-30. Concludes that through his insistence on maintaining the Antilles under French authority, Césaire severely limited his idea of negritude to the point that nothing valuable came out of it for the Antilles.

Finkelstein, Haim N. *Surrealism and the Crisis of the Object.* Ann Arbor, Mich.: University Microcosm International, 1979. Chapters on love and the object and on the occult and the object are useful.

Fox, Hugh, ed. *First Fire: Central and South American Indian Poetry.* Garden City, N.Y.: Anchor Press/Doubleday, 1978. An anthology of this body of poetry.

Frobenius, Leo. *The Childhood of Man.* New York: Meridian Books, 1960. Civilization studied from the perspective of this great anthropologist who so influenced Césaire and his coterie.

Frutkin, Susan. *Aimé Césaire: Black between Worlds.* Washington, D.C.: Center for Advanced International Studies, 1973. The focus here is on Césaire as part Western, part African, part European. Lengthy discussion of his views on communism.

Fuyet, Hervé, et al. "Décolonisation et classes sociales dans *La Tragédie du roi Christophe.*" *French Review* 46, no. 6 (May 1973): 1101ff. Looks at class stratification and decolonization as depicted in *Christophe.*

Hale, Thomas A. *Les Ecrits d'Aimé Césaire: Bibliographie commentée.* Montreal: Les Presses de l'Université de Montréal, 1978. Special issue of *Etudes françaises* 14, nos. 3-4 (1978). Indispensable bibliography of Césaire's writings, with helpful commentary on revisions and other circumstances of publication.

―――. "Structural Dynamics in a Third World Classic: Aimé Césaire's *Cahier d'un retour au pays natal.*" *Yale French Studies* 53 (1976): 163-74. A look at how structure functions in the *Cahier.*

―――. "Sur *Une tempête* d'Aimé Césaire." *Etudes littéraires* 6, no. 1 (April 1973): 21-35. One of the few studies of this curious play; worth reading.

―――. "Two Decades, Four Versions: The Evolution of Aimé Césaire's *Cahier d'un retour au pays natal.*" In *When the Drumbeat Changes,* 186-95. Washington, D.C.: Three Continents Press, 1981. A useful analysis of how Césaire revised *Cahier* over a two-year period.

Hamilton, Russell G. *Voices from an Empire.* Minneapolis: University of Minnesota Press, 1975. A thorough analysis of Lusophone African literature up to 1974.

Harris, Rodney E. *L'Humanisme dans le théâtre d'Aimé Césaire.* Sherbrooke, Canada: Editions Naaman, 1973. A book of questionable merit, meticulously studied and severely criticized by Christophe Dailly.

―――. "The Scrupulous Aimé Césaire." *Cahiers césairiens* 2 (Fall 1975): 25-28. How Césaire's changes to his work show him to be an "indefatigable worker." Reasons cited for changes to *Une saison au Congo* are self-evident.

―――. "The English Translations of Césaire's Theater." *Cahiers césairiens* 1 (Spring 1974): 32-34. A review of the translations of *Une saison* and *Christophe,* showing the problem of establishing the texts because of Césaire's many revisions.

Hawkins, Hunt. "Aimé Césaire's Lesson about Decolonization in *La Tragédie du roi Christophe.*" *Quarterly of the College Language Association* 30, no. 2 (December 1986): 144-54.

Jahn, Janheiz. *Muntu.* New York: Grove Press, 1968. In this pivotal but now widely rejected book, Jahn advances the theories of Nommo.

_____. *Neo-African Literature.* New York: Grove Press, 1968.

Johnson, Lemuel. *Highlife for Caliban.* Ann Arbor, Mich.: Ardis Publishers, 1973. Poems by this Liberian poet, better known for his critical works on African literature.

Joppa, Francis Anani. *L'Engagement des écrivains africains noirs de langue française.* Sherbrooke, Canada: Editions Naaman, 1982. How the Sartrean concept of *engagement* works in Francophone African writers.

Juin, Hubert. *Aimé Césaire, poète noir.* Paris: Présence Africaine, 1956. A short pioneering look at Césaire, now outdated.

_____. "Le Songe de Toussaint Louverture." *Présence africaine* 16 (October-November 1953): 83-88.

Kesteloot, Lilyan. *Anthologie négro-africaine.* Verviers, Belgium: Marabout Université/Editions Verviers, 1967. Excellent short "notice" on Césaire, with a somewhat questionable list of the "principal symbols" used by the poet, and with selections from the *Cahier, Soleil cou coupé, Discours sur le colonialisme,* and *Lettre à Maurice Thorez.*

_____. *Comprendre le "Cahier d'un retour au pays natal" d'Aimé Césaire.* Paris: Saint Paul/Classiques Africaines, 1982. An analysis of the *Cahier* to assist the reader in understanding this work.

_____. "Première Lecture d'un poème de C., 'Batouque.'" *Etudes littéraires* 6, no. 1 (April 1973): 49-71.

_____. "*La Tragédie du roi Christophe* ou les indépendances africaines au miroir d'Haiti." *Présence africaine,* no. 51 (Third Trimester 1964): 131-45. Translated in *Présence africaine* [English ed.] 23, no. 51 (1964): 123-29.

Kesteloot, Lilyan, and B[arthélemy] Kotchy. *Aimé Césaire, l'homme et l'oeuvre.* Paris: Présence Africaine, 1973. One of the most important studies of Césaire.

Killam, G. D., ed. *African Writers on African Writing.* Evanston, Ill.: Northwestern University Press, 1973. An anthology of commentary on the processes of writing as viewed by African writers.

Laroche, Maximilien. "*La Tragédie du roi Christophe* du point de vue de l'histoire d'Haïti." *Etudes littéraires* 6, no. 1 (April 1973): 36-48. An important analysis of Christophe's character.

Larrier, Renée. "Racism in the United States: An Issue in Caribbean Poetry." *Journal of Caribbean Studies* (Spring 1981): 51-71.

Legum, Colin. *Pan-Africanism: A Short Political Guide.* New York: Praeger, 1965. Provides background to the concept of pan Africanism.

Leiner, Jacqueline. "Césaire et les problèmes du langage chez un écrivain francophone." *Esprit créateur* 17, no. 2 (Summer 1977): 133-42. Dexterously demonstrates how Césaire uses French and language in general in his poetry.

_____. "Entretien avec A.C." In *Tropiques*, vol. 1, pp. v-xxiv, edited by Aimé Césaire. Paris: Jean-Michel Place, 1978.

_____, ed. *Soleil éclaté.* Tübinger: Gunter Narr Verlag, 1984. Contains literary and scholarly pieces by some 40 persons, published in honor of Césaire's seventieth birthday.

Ménil, René. "Le Romanesque et le réalisme dans *La Tragédie du roi Christophe.*" *Action* [Martinique], January 1965. Looks at the question of what we might call mimesis in *Christophe*.

Michel, Jean-Claude. *Les Ecrivains noirs et le surréalisme.* Sherbrooke, Canada: Editions Naaman, 1982. Indispensable section on Césaire as a surrealist.

Ngal, Georges. "Chronologie de la vie d'A.C." *Présence francophone* 3 (Fall 1971): 163-66. An abbreviated chronology.

_____. "L'image et l'enracinement chez A. C." *Présence francophone* 6 (Spring 1973): 5-28. Contends that the vegetable imagery in Césaire is not gratuitous. Especially useful for its analysis of sun imagery.

Ngal, Mbawil a Mpaang [Georges]. *Aimé Césaire: Un homme à la recherche d'une patrie.* 1975. Dakar, Abidjan: Nouvelles Editions Africaines, 1983. Intellectual biography of Césaire, 1913-46.

Ngaté, Jonathan. "'Mauvais sang' de Rimbaud et *Cahier d'un retour au pays natal* de Césaire: La poésie au service de la révolution." *Cahiers césairiens* 3 (Spring 1977): 25-32. Shows how revolution functions in Rimbaud and how Rimbaud influenced Césaire.

_____. *Francophone African Fiction: Reading a Literary Tradition.* Trenton, N.J.: Africa World Press, 1988. A book-length study of the fiction of Francophone Africa, but one in which Césaire is mentioned more than once.

_____. "Maryse Condé: Césaire's *Cahier.*" *Cahiers césairiens* 4 (Fall 1980): 13-15. Crucial review of Condé's study.

Nisbet, Anne Marie, et al. Preface to *Négritude et antillanité: Etude d'"Une tempête" d'Aimé Césaire.* Kensington: New South Wales University Press, 1982. A rare look at *Une tempête* from the perspective of negritude.

Nkosi, Lewis. *Tasks and Masks.* Harlow, Essex: Longman House, 1981. Césaire's role in negritude and modernism.

Ntonfo, André. *L'Homme et l'identité dans le roman des Antilles et Guyane françaises.* Sherbrooke, Canada: Editions Naaman, 1982. Although concerned with identity in prose works of the Antilles, looks at this key problem in relation to Césaire.

_____. "Jalons pour une autonomie de la littérature antillaise." *Présence francophone* 22 (Spring 1981): 141-56. Differentiates African and Caribbean negritude; considers Daniel Boukman's critiques of Césaire and Glissant's and Zobel's concepts of the past.

Odden, Marcel. "Les Tragédies de la décolonisation." In *Le Théâtre moderne depuis la deuxième guerre mondiale.* Paris: CNRS, 1967. Studies the most important of Césaire's dramatic themes, decolonization.

Ormerod, Beverley. *An Introduction to the French Caribbean Novel.* London: Heinemann, 1985.

Owusu-Sarpong, Albert. *Le Temps historique dans l'oeuvre théâtrale d'Aimé Césaire.* Sherbrooke, Canada: Editions Naaman, 1986. How time functions, especially historical time, in Césaire's dramatic works.

Pallister, Janis L. *The Aesthetics of Anger: African Poetry Today.* Bowling Green, Ohio: Bowling Green State University Press, 1980. How anger forms an aesthetic in modern Francophone black poetry; Césaire included.

_____. "Historical Figures as *Exempla* in the Work of Aimé Césaire." *French Literature Series* 7 (1981): 124-29. How Toussaint and Lumumba present role models.

_____. "Island Imagery in the Poetry of Sao Tomé, Cape Verde, Madagascar, and Mauritius." Paper presented at African Literature Association meeting, Boone, North Carolina, April 1978. The use of the island as metaphor in the geographical areas mentioned, with applications for Martinique and Guadeloupe.

_____. "Lamine Diakhaté and the Modern French Poets." *French Review* 55, no. 6 (May 1982): 770-79. The role of woman in Diakhaté's poetry as compared and contrasted with poets of the Metropole.

_____. "Time, Tense, and Tempo in the Work of Jean Dieudonné Garçon." *Esprit créateur* 17, no. 2 (Summer 1977): 159-67. How these three things function in terms of the rhythm, with implications regarding rhythm and colonization of Haiti for Césaire's work.

Pestre de Almeida, Lilian. "Le Bestiaire symbolique dans *Une saison au Congo.*" *Présence francophone* 13 (Fall 1976): 93-105. The symbolism of animals in *Une saison,* theriomorphic ones in particular.

_____. "Les Deux textes de *Et les chiens se taisaient.*" *Oeuvres et critiques* 4, no. 1 (Fall 1979): 203-11. Like Harris and Hale, studies revisions, here of *Et les chiens se taisaient,* from its first appearance in *Les Armes miraculeuses* to its independent publication.

_____. "Un puzzle poétique. Introduction à une analyse dans *Une tempête* de Césaire." *Présence francophone* 14 (Spring 1977): 121-32. Views the play as a game, or a jigsaw puzzle, in which Shakespeare's scenes and episodes have been cut up and inverted and must be "reassembled" in order to make a picture, different from the original. Uses Baudelaire and Freud, but Shakespeare only very little, and in translation.

_____. "Rire haitien, rire africain (le comique dans *La Tragédie du roi Christophe* de Césaire)." *Présence francophone* 10 (Spring 1975): 59-71. How laughter as a manifestation of African and Caribbean personality functions in *Christophe* (in which the humor is problematic).

_____. "'Les Structures anthropologiques de l'imaginaire' dans un texte de Césaire." *Présence francophone* 2, no. 3 (Fall 1981): 143-61. Using Gilbert Durand, this article claims to be a methodical exploration of symbolism in *Cahier,* bringing to bear other poems by Césaire, as well as Sartre's "Orphée noir" and Jahn's *Muntu,* both viewed as simplifications, and even using biblical passage intertextually. How article is "anthropological" is not that clear.

_____. *O Teatro negro de Aimé Césaire.* Rio de Janeiro: UFF-CEUFF, 1978. Contains six essays on Césaire's theater.

Pigeon, Gérard Georges. "Interview avec Aimé Césaire à Fort-de-France, le 12 janvier 1977." *Cahiers césairiens* 3 (Spring 1977): 1-6. Again a conversation with Césaire in which his writings and his concept of the writer are discussed.

_____. "Le Rôle des termes médicaux, de bestiaire et de la flore dans l'imagerie césairienne." *Cahiers césairiens* 3 (Spring 1977): 7-24. How medical, animal, and vegetable terms are used in metaphorical ways by Césaire.

Poésie du monde noir. Paris: Hatier, 1973. Anthology of black poetry with translations from Harlem Renaissance poets, but not from Spanish or Portuguese. Selections from the *Cahier* and *Ferrements.* Views Césaire's poetry as extremely difficult but "authentic" and Césaire as occupying an eminent place in "the negro-african world."

Régis, Antoine. *Les Ecrivains français et les Antilles: Des premiers pères blancs aux surréalistes noirs.* Paris: Maisonneuve et Larose, 1979. Relationships between metropolitan poets and those of the Antilles.

Renan, Ernest. *Oeuvres complètes,* edited by Henriette Psichari. Vol. 3. Paris: Calmann-Lévy, 1949. Contains the important *Avenir de la science,* with ideas on progress and race that were carefully read and refuted by negritude writers. Also contains *Caliban.*

Richard, René. "Césaire et Shakespeare." In *Actes du Colloque d'Abidjan,* 122-34. Paris: Présence Africaine, 1971.

Salien, Jean-Marie. "Négritude et lutte des classes dans *La Tragédie du roi Christophe* d'Aimé Césaire: Essai de sociocritique." *Présence franco-*

phone 24 (Spring 1982): 147-55. Uses a sociological approach and applies the theories of Lucien Goldmann to study *Christophe*.

Sartre, Jean-Paul. "Orphée Noir." Preface to *Anthologie de la nouvelle poésie nègre et malgache*, edited by Léopold Sédar Senghor. 1948. Paris: Presses Universitaires Françaises, 1972. A pivotal essay; widely referenced and ultimately put to serious question.

_____. "The Political Thought of Patrice Lumumba." *Présence africaine* [English ed.] 47, no. 19 (Third Quarter 1963): 58-97.

Scharfman, Ronnie L. *"Engagement" and the Language of the Subject in the Poetry of Aimé Césaire*. Gainesville: University Presses of Florida, 1987. A sometimes simplistic, sometimes overly nuanced study of Césaire's language of commitment and the role of subject as subject and subject as object.

Sellin, Eric. *"Négritude:* Status or Dynamics?" *Esprit créateur* 10, no. 3 (Fall 1970): 163-81. A discussion of the pros and cons of negritude and how it might function in a literary text.

_____. "'Soleil cou coupé.'" *Romance Notes* 14, no. 1 (Autumn 1972): 13-16. A very brief analysis of the image of the sun in this poem.

Senghor, Léopold Sédar. *Anthologie de la nouvelle poésie nègre et malgache*. 1948. Paris: Presses Universitaires Françaises, 1972. The first important anthology of the negritude movement, including poets from Africa, the Antilles, and Madagascar.

_____. *Elégies majeures*. Paris: Seuil, 1979. Collected elegies of Senghor.

_____. "La Révolution de 1889 et Léo Frobenius." *Ethiopiques* 30 (1982): 5-16. An important article on this anthropologist whose theories were so important to the negritude poets, especially those expressed in his *Histoire de la civilisation africaine*.

_____. *Liberté 1: Négritude et humanisme*. Paris: Seuil, 1964. Philosophical writings.

_____. *Liberté 2: Nation et voie africaine du socialisme*. Paris: Seuil, 1971. Philosophical and political writings.

_____. *Liberté 3: Négritude et civilisation de l'universel*. Paris: Seuil, 1977. Philosophical and political writings that embrace the theories of Teilhard de Chardin's noosphere.

_____. *Poèmes*. 1953. Paris: Seuil, 1973. Collected poems, excluding his elegies.

Shungu, Ekanga. "La Bibliothèque de Maryse Condé." *Jeune afrique*, 25 April 1984, 66-67. Specific reference is made to Césaire in this study of Condé.

Snyder, Emile. "A Reading of Aimé Césaire's *Return to My Native Land. Esprit créateur* 10, no. 3 (Fall 1970): 197-212. One of the first analyses of the *Cahier* by an American writer. Now somewhat dated.

Songolo, Aliko. *Aimé Césaire, une poétique de la découverte.* Paris: L'Harmattan, 1985. A sensitive study.

_____. *"Cadastre* et *Ferrements* de Césaire: Une nouvelle poétique pour une nouvelle politique." *Esprit créateur* 17 (Summer 1977): 143-59. Shows the irony residing in the fact that, although critics always contend that Césaire is first and foremost a poet, even in his drama, critics nonetheless do not study his poetry as much as they do his drama.

_____. "Surrealism and Black Literatures in French." *French Review* 55, no. 6 (May 1982): 724-32.

Traoré, Bakary. "Le Théâtre africain: Réalités et perspectives." In *Actes du Colloque d'Abidjan.* Paris: Présence Africaine, 1971.

Tribble, Keith O. "La Réception des oeuvres des fondateurs de la négritude en URSS." *Oeuvres et critiques* 3, no. 2, and 4, no. 1 (Fall 1979): 65-72. Critical reception of negritude writers in the Soviet Union.

Trouillet, Henock. *Le Gouvernement du roi Henri Christophe.* Port-au-Prince, Haiti: Imprimerie Centrale, 1974. Useful historical background to Césaire's play.

Visage, Bertrand. "Aimé Césaire." In *Dictionnaire des littératures de langue française,* edited by Jean-Pierre Beaumarchais. Paris: Bordas, 1984. Short entry, but of interest for its claims.

Wagner, Jean. *Black Poets of the United States.* Urbana: University of Illinois Press, 1973. Mentions relationships between African-American and Francophone black poets.

Walker, Keith Louis. *La Cohésion poétique de l'oeuvre césairienne.* Tübingen: Gunter Narr Verlag; Paris: Editions Jean-Michel Place, 1979. Attempts to show that Césaire's poetic metaphors are coherent, so that his literary output is a *Gesamtkunstwerk.* Fails, however, to see duality of some of these metaphors.

Warner, Keith Q. *Voix françaises du monde noir.* New York: Holt, Rinehart & Winston, 1971. The passage from *Une saison au Congo* includes Lumumba's famous speech, with exercises for the intermediate-level student.

Zadi-Zaourou, Bernard. *Césaire entre deux cultures.* Dakar: Nouvelles Editions Africains, 1978. Césaire as a cultural métis.

Index

The Author

Janis L. Pallister is Distinguished University Professor Emeritus of Romance Languages at Bowling Green State University. She received her Ph.D. from the University of Minnesota in 1964 and has served on the faculties of Colby and Black Hills colleges. Her publications include translations of Antoine Bolamba's *Esanzo* and the poems of Césaire and others in *The Bruised Reed*, for which she received the Columbia University Translation Center Award in 1978. She serves on the editorial board of *Revue francophone* and has received the Ohio Education Association's Human Relations Commission Award (1979) and a National Endowment for the Humanities grant (1980). She is currently writing a book on Quebec cinema with the support of a senior fellowship from the Canadian Embassy (1989-90) and a National Endowment for the Humanities grant (1990)

The Editor

David O'Connell is professor of foreign languages and chair of the Department of Foreign Languages at Georgia State University. He received his Ph.D. from Princeton University in 1966, where he was a National Woodrow Wilson Fellow, the Bergen Fellow in Romance Languages, and a National Woodrow Wilson Dissertation Fellow. He is the author of *The Teachings of Saint Louis: A Critical Text* (1972), *Les Propos de Saint Louis* (1974), *Louis-Ferdinand Céline* (1976), *The Instructions of Saint Louis: A Critical Text* (1979), and *Michel de Saint Pierre: A Catholic Novelist at the Crossroads* (1990). He is the editor of *Catholic Writers in France since 1945* (1983) and has served as review editor (1977-79) and managing editor (1987-90) of the *French Review*.